A CURiOUS CHiLDHOOD?

To Meriet,
Hope you enjoy!
Helen Levy

A CURiOUS CHiLDHOOD?

What do you think?

Fran Levy

Contents

Contents

Contents

Acknowledgment

My thanks go to all those who have contributed to my journey in getting this book off the ground and into their hands.

Firstly, Rob and Jan, who unwittingly sowed the seed together on the same day yet have never met.

Nick, Roger, Sally and Jemitra for their support with my cover development.

Wye Media for just being ready with valuable expertise when needed to put the finishing touches to the cover.

Pam, who willingly lent her ear and thoughts from start to finish.

Equally important are my thanks to my 26 readers who read as I wrote, from day one in February 2021, displaying such encouraging enthusiasm.

INTRODUCTION

My father, an only son, was very shy. He had one older sister.

His father was in the tobacco trade, commuting by train daily into London.

My father was academic but his mother would not agree to his going to London University. She didn't want him to leave home. He became a schoolmaster.

Apart from his love of history, which was his subject, he played cricket and tennis passionately.

My mother's parents were from "gentleman farmer" stock. Both families, living within the Canterbury area, had inherited resources. They were founder members of the Shire Horse Society.

Her mother attended the Royal School of Needlework "finishing school", where she embroidered part of the front panel of Queen Mary's wedding dress.

My mother was creative too, as was her mother's side of the family. Her cousin became a renowned film producer of WW11 films. She always took great pride in his achievements.

In the 1940s, my father was evacuated with pupils from London to the Canterbury area of Kent. While in

Canterbury, he joined the cricket and tennis community. My mother's family moved in the same circles.

Her family having their own grass court meant he was invited to play tennis and have tea, joining my mother and her three sisters.

During the war, my father served in the Air Force as a PT instructor to rehabilitate servicemen suffering psychologically from their war experience. He was posted to Kashmir, India.

Before the end of the war, a Church of England marriage was arranged, though my father was a recognised agnostic. (His church interest was purely architectural.)

They soon produced three children between 1944 and 1948. Three girls.

Let my story unfold.

Chapter A The Avenue

A1 Life's Priorities

7 Farringdon Avenue is a semi-detached house. It has a short drive.

The Austin 7 can be pulled up off the road between iron gates; there's no garage. The drive slopes slightly from the front door before it reaches the pavement. A single wooden block is in the centre of the drive to bolt each gate closed. The gates can be used independently if needed, without the other one swinging open.

I'm not allowed to swing on the gates but find times when I think I can do it unnoticed.

An elderly man, Mr Harper, lives next door with his wife. Their home is smaller than ours as it has no upstairs. He isn't around very often as he has difficulty walking; I don't think he would be around to tell on me. His wife is around even less.

Our gates are patterned in twisted iron. The pattern meets the top rung, then goes down to meet the bottom rung. My feet are small enough to tuck between the patterns. By holding onto the top rung, I can swing from open to closed, down the slope to the block.

There's nothing that matches the feeling I get. I dare not do it more than once at a time; there's a clatter when it reaches the block, which stops the gate dead in its tracks. I'm glad the block is there, otherwise I would swing out onto the pavement where I could be seen.

All the houses in the road have back gardens. We have a few chickens at the bottom of ours.

My father is visiting Mr Harper's back garden; he enters from the front. I ask to go too. We go down the side of his house through a low gate. It's the roses at the back I like to see most because they are a mass of colour.

Strangely, the roses bloom on top of posts, not like ours which are bushes near the ground or hanging from walls.

There's a row of these posts. Because the roses bloom high up, he can see them while he's sitting down indoors; the blooms are higher than the window sill, so he can look out and enjoy them.

He tells me they are called standard roses. Mr Harper can smell the roses without bending down, but my nose isn't high enough. I'd like to be lifted up, but I never ask as I would have to stop them talking.

There is another neighbour I visit with my mother. She lives further down on our side of the road. The two women chat inside the house, never in the garden.

Mr Harper and my father always chat in the garden, never inside the house.

My mother often puts the pram out in the back garden close to the house so that my new baby sister can sleep in the fresh air. My mother keeps her eye on the pram while she is busy inside. The pram has its hood up and is covered with a net to stop Tommy, our long-haired cat, climbing in with her. Tommy loves to sleep where it is warm and cosy.

Opposite my house lives a boy with a collection of wonderful toys. I love his low trolley filled with little wooden milk bottles painted white. He can pull it around his house and deliver the milk wherever he wants.

He allows me to load and unload the bottles, but I don't deliver them around his house; only he does that. He also has brightly coloured square blocks, which I can pile into a tower. If I'm very, very careful, I can build it high.

When he's out of the room delivering, I play with his toys on my own.

He's older than me. I don't go to play there unless my older sister is visiting; this is because I'd have to cross the road.

I've come out our back door, at the side of our house. I'm just in time to see my sister crossing the road to go and visit.

Why hasn't she taken me? I know that she will soon be let in through his front door; it will then be shut and I will be left on the wrong side. I won't be able to reach the knocker.

I don't hesitate.

I run as fast as I can to reach the door before it's shut on me.

Wham!

I don't reach the door, not even his gate.

I'm on the ground, dazed; hit by a bicycle. I'm shocked: the road felt empty.

I plead with the cyclist.

"Please don't tell anyone."

I'm overcome with worry at what I did and fear that my mother or father will find out that I crossed the road without looking first for any traffic.

The gates were open; I didn't give the road a single thought as my mind was only on playing with the boy's milk bottles.

A2 Instructions Delivered

Over the road, the boy lets me pack and unpack his milk bottles, but I can't wheel the cart out of the room as he does. My older sister is over here with us; he has books she likes to read.

Some of his toys are much smaller: little lorries and racing cars that he can push up a ramp into a little shed that his dad made for him. There is also an ambulance in the shed that he says will ring its bell loudly if any of his cars are in a crash.

I listen to everything he says:

"If you ever see an ambulance you must run and hide."

Swinging on the gate, I'm keeping my eyes on the top road. I'm enjoying the feeling, but I'm anxious about my father possibly returning home. I can see the bigger street from where he will turn down into our smaller road. He never comes in from the left, so I don't ever look that way when I'm on the gate.

An ambulance comes from the left. It takes me by surprise; it wasn't ringing its bell.

I'm off the gate and in through the back door to get under the kitchen table. I stay quietly, my heart beating. Was I fast enough? Will the men come up our drive and get me? I'm too scared to come out.

I think they may still be waiting for me by the gate. How long do I have to stay hidden? How long before I am safe? The boy didn't tell me that.

My mother has found me. She laughs.

"It's his antics, that's all."

I'm not swinging on the gate this time; I'm crossing the road with my sister just in front of me. We've been at the boy's house and are on our way back across the road.

Up on the big street, I see a light flashing; it's an ambulance. I make a sudden dash to reach my hiding place under the table, but I trip on the wooden block sticking up.

I didn't reach my hiding place this time.

A small deckchair with its bright striped canvas is brought out and unfolded on the drive. I have to sit for a while quietly until I say yes to the question:

"Have you stopped seeing stars?"

At bedtime, I ask for my favourite book. It's called, *Whose Little Bird am I?* I can't read the words but join in with them as I know the book by heart. I can follow the pictures:

"Am I your little bird?"

"You are not my little bird; your neck is too long," said the pigeon.

I think about the poor little bird searching for its mother. I'm happy when he finds her. My bad trip is forgotten.

A3 Thwarted Plans

The room where I hid under the table has a small window. The table has a white enamel top. Sometimes the mincer is fixed to the table. Leftovers from the Sunday joint are wound through the mincer and will later be made into shepherd's pie.

The table is the main piece of furniture in the kitchen, apart from a cupboard with a pull-down enamelled shelf. Its doors are too near the floor for me to crawl under.

In the front room, the biggest piece of furniture is the settee; it has two matching arm chairs. They have broad, flat arms. I'm allowed to sit on these arms. I sometimes climb up onto the back, which is also wide and flat. Tommy claws at the rust-coloured uncut moquette. He likes the front of the arms best.

Sometimes, I can tell he has come into the front room only to claw at the settee. He goes straight to the same arm. It now feels soft and furry to touch, unlike the rest of the settee which is hard and rough.

A man has come to our house to take our photograph. We three sisters sit on the settee in a row. We are all dressed up, with me in the middle.

While setting up his things ready to take the photograph, the man chats to us about our settee:

"We have a settee with an arm that looks like yours. Our cat goes for the arm, just like yours does."

I'm thinking our cats must know each other. I've heard adults say "copy-cat".

My older sister's school is not far away. I've often walked there with my mother to meet her at the gate.

My plan is to put my doll in its pushchair and go to meet my sister as I know the way.

I'm soon ready to set off.

I turn right out of the gate, turn left at the top by the big street and follow the pavement around the large green park. I will soon see the school up ahead on my left. I will wait by the school gate until she comes out. When she sees me, we will walk home together.

I've not quite reached the school when a car pulls up behind me. I turn to look. I'm very surprised to see a car the same as ours.

I stare. Is it? It's my father's car. Why is it here? Where is he going?

Along with my doll and the pushchair, I'm bundled onto the back seat and driven straight back home; he doesn't even wait for my sister to come out.

I was so near; at least he could have waited till I reached the school gates.

Chapter B The Close

B1 Boundaries Learnt

We've now moved to 6 Ash Close. It's a quiet area like Farringdon Avenue; a similar style of semi-detached house but with more garden, a garage and numerous garden sheds. Also, it is much closer to the town.

Our new home is at the far end of Ash Close; it's at the top of the lollipop-shaped road. We have a small gate near the far end of the back garden which leads into a builder's yard. We are allowed to walk through the yard; this way we can reach the town of Petts Wood very quickly.

I've seen people pass through our garden; otherwise, it's a long walk around many streets for them to reach the shops. Mostly I see an elderly man using a walking stick going through our garden. He goes up through it, but I never see him come back.

We are lucky to have this little gate. Our garden is shaped like a pixie cap: a little farther on past the gate, it ends in a point.

We have lawns, apple trees, blackcurrant and gooseberry bushes, a small Victoria plum tree, not much taller than my father, and a peach tree growing against the five-foot fence that separates our garden from our neighbour's.

The small triangle of garden beyond the gate is left wild, growing a few small trees and bushes. The compost heap is hidden in it. My father grows tulips in the back garden; at the front, rose bushes between crazy paving.

Father's parents live in Bickley on the same train line as Petts Wood. My mother's family lives in Wingham, a small village near Canterbury. Two of her sisters, Jean and Dulcie, live at home; both are younger than my mother.

Both my grandparents' homes have walk-in larders. One is at Windyridge, Wingham, the other in Bickley. The layout of the larders is the same in both places.

There is also a larder at Ash Close, but it is in the kitchen, not off the passageway, as in my grandparents' homes.

The door of each larder opens outward with standing space inside where you can spin round to find all you want on the surrounding shelves. They each have a small window to the outdoors covered with a fine metal mesh to stop insects flying in. A white marble shelf runs around level with the adult's waist; this "cold shelf" has on it cheese, eggs and sometimes cooked meats like at the butcher's.

Both the marble and the fresh air keep the tiny room cool. The straight-up wooden door to each larder is to stop warm air in the house getting inside the larder. The tiny metal latches on the doors are on the left high up, well out of my reach. I would need a chair to stand on, so I'm never sent to fetch anything.

I'm not interested enough in the contents of the larders to ever want to go into them. There are lots of jars and large tins with tight fitting lids. Windyridge has a big old square biscuit tin that is fetched out sometimes; Bickley has a small lidded biscuit barrel, kept on the kitchen table.

The lovely biscuits down at Windyridge are made in the Rayburn, which is always hot, winter and summer; it's kept stoked by grandad. Bickley biscuits are usually rich tea or Scotch shortbread.

There are no sweets at Windyridge.

At Bickley there is always an amber cut-glass dish of sweets on the low oblong coffee table in the front room where the television sits on a tall cupboard. Its glass front is square and greenish; it's never on.

The sweets are wrapped in bright, shining paper; the long ones look like tiny Christmas crackers. I'm puzzled as to why they are there, and who they are for. In all my trips to Bickley, I've never been offered one; nor do I see anyone else offered them. They go down, only to be filled up again. I never see who fills them, nor who eats them.

Humbugs, dolly-mixtures and jelly-babies are sometimes shared, but they are not in the glass dish. Smarties are my favourite. I like the look of their perfect shape and smooth, even colours. I like to suck away the hard coating to reach the soft chocolate; then to eat it all by itself.

Bickley is in a terrace; all have very small front gardens. A short brick wall runs all along the pavement in front of the row; there are also short walls that divide each garden from its neighbour.

Encaustic tiles of red, cream and black run up the short paths to the front doors; all are arranged in the same pattern. The houses in the row are all identical. Each has a strong, spacious, wooden porch with a front door that has an oval window high up. The downstairs windows in the row all have a band of patterned coloured glass above where you look out.

Grandma's front door has a striped canvas screen you pull across when the sun is out so that its paint can always look fresh. The houses in the row have pleasant features and are nicely proportioned. They are small, happy-looking places on the outside.

My Bickley grandparents have plenty of light coming into the back of their house; a large area of windows gives an excellent view of their back garden. There's a long narrow window-sill, level with my waist; on it stands a full row of potted fuchsia cuttings. All are equally distanced, with the cuttings all the same height. At the end of the long row is a jam jar of water holding more cuttings.

The flowers in the garden are very neat. The grass never seems to grow; it never touches the flowers in the border. The tight little flower bunches are arranged blue then orange like a neat necklace around the lawn. It's not a garden for children; not even the wind seems to get the chance to untidy it.

A slatted fence surrounds the garden. I've never seen anyone in it either working or sitting. I study it from the long window, looking out above the row of cuttings on the sill, usually when grandma is setting tea.

I'd like to see inside the small, neat shed but I never ask to do that while at Bickley. I would ask at Windyridge quite happily without even thinking about it. I don't think I would be allowed to walk across the grass here.

On the Bickley table, grandma places the aluminium black-handled teapot with its delicate design pressed into it; there is a matching little jug and sugar bowl with a pair of tiny silver tongs like the large ones at home that are used to sort the coals in the fire.

The bowl is not topped up from the blue bag of loose sugar filled at the grocers. There are no grains of sugar here that I can see. There are perfect white cubes that I've seen some people on holiday pick up and suck. These cubes come packed in a small cube-shaped box; the lid slides up to show the tidy sugar cubes inside, perfectly set so that I can't see the joins between the cubes until they are lifted out.

B2 Additional Bonus?

When I move my tongue around inside my mouth, the front teeth feel different. My new front teeth are slowly growing, to replace my baby teeth, but they don't have much room.

I'm thinking I must look a bit like a strange creature.

I can look in the bathroom cabinet mirror by reaching up on a stool. In my parents' bedroom, there is a utility dressing table that has one big mirror at the back with smaller wing mirrors, one on either side, hinged so that they can flap about. The mirror must think it's a bird; I don't know why it's been given these wings.

I don't go into my parents' bedroom at the back of the house very often. Now I'm here looking at my four front teeth; it's a strange sight. I don't know anyone else with teeth like mine.

Some children have a big gap where two teeth used to be. I've never had gaps as my two front teeth have never come out.

Eating an apple when a tooth wobbles about has always worked before but not with my front ones; they stay stuck in place. My new ones on either side of them can't find any space. Four teeth look very strange; my front teeth have grown wings!

My mother is taking me to the dentist. I wonder what he will say when he sees my wings. Will he find them amusing?

"We'll have to take the old two out to make room for the new ones, otherwise they will be crooked when the old ones drop out."

Will I be able to have them for the tooth fairy, I wonder? Perhaps it's cheating if they didn't drop out?

The large mask goes on. I breathe and smell the strange gas; I feel myself slip into deep sleep. It's a pleasant feeling as I like slipping to sleep.

The dentist hands me my two teeth. I feel lucky to have two to go under my pillow tonight. Two wishes!

Will it work?

B3 Observing Behaviour

We sometimes drive to Wallingford to stay with uncle John and aunty Sheila. Aunty Sheila is my father's older sister. He has no brothers, just one sister. She is married to uncle John, a vicar. They live in a very big house; the rooms all have very tall ceilings. The Vicarage has large surrounding gardens, which are well kept but not perfect like at Bickley.

They have two boys, much older than us. I don't really know them, even though at times all the family stays at Ash Close with us. When they do, lots of camping beds have to be put up in our big front bedroom. "It's like a dormitory," my father says, laughing.

Outside the back kitchen door of the Vicarage stands a very large wooden barrel. It's taller than me. A drainpipe runs down the wall from the huge gutters of the house into the barrel so that it can catch the rain water.

All the adults are relaxing in deck chairs just beyond the backdoor. This area is paved with large, flat stones which run along the back of the house, with the gardens laid out beyond. A low table has been brought out of the Vicarage to stand between the adults. A tea tray is brought out and the cups arranged on their saucers around the table so they can all be reached.

It's a lovely sunny afternoon. I have a low, rush-seated stool to sit on. I can't easily practise my yo-yo sitting down, so I'm standing to get a better chance to get it right.

A man appears from around the corner of the Vicarage. He doesn't acknowledge the adults as he approaches.

Uncle John rises quickly after spotting him; they are both near me. My curiosity has stopped me yo-yo-ing. I look up at them while a few words are whispered.

I catch uncle John saying, "I'll deal with it." The man hands over a small cloth bundle and leaves.

I hear that it contains kittens because the bundle is meowing. Perhaps vicars look after little homeless creatures?

Before I have more time to think, uncle John's hand, still holding the kittens in the cloth, moves over the top of the barrel a few feet from me. I stare at his hand with the bundle, puzzled by what he is doing.

Pulling his hand away he now holds an empty cloth; the kittens are gone.

Stuffing the cloth quickly between the barrel and the wall he returns to his deckchair to finish his tea, quickly picking up the adult conversation.

Nothing is mentioned. They all chat and laugh as if nothing has happened. Uncle John carries on just as before.

I'm in silent shock and turmoil by what my uncle John just did; there's no one here I want to talk to. Nobody cared enough to move from their deckchairs to save the kittens.

B4 Curiosity's Consequence

Today, at home, I find a suitcase packed; it's standing in the hallway.

Is someone leaving?

"You are going to spend some nights at grandma's, Poppet, while Mummy is away."

I feel drained by the thought. I've never stayed at grandma's. There's never been the need as Bickley isn't far away. Why is my father sending me to sleep there?

"Mummy is in hospital."

My father drives to Bickley to drop me off. I am wearing my favourite coat: deep pink tweed with a dark brown velvet collar and four large matching velvet buttons arranged in a square. Dressed in it, I feel confident.

I will put on a brave face though Bickley is the last place I want to be sent to sleep. I've not started school yet, so I will be in the Bickley house all day long.

I will have to go upstairs to sleep, so I might have to pass the long box in the hallway at the top of the landing. Draped over it is a faded Union Jack. It's a very big flag so it hangs over the sides of the box with its corners touching the floor. It can be hung on special days from a white flag pole which can be reached from the front bedroom window. The pole sticks out of the house wall above the tiled porch roof.

The box with the old draped flag is like a coffin; it gives me the creeps. I see it through the bannisters when I go up to use the toilet; I try not to look.

I don't like the bathroom, either. The large, thick tiles, cream and dark green, go right to the ceiling, just like the lavatories in Bromley Park. The big cream wash basin on a large, square, cream stand has bulky, ugly taps. The window is high up so not even an adult can look out.

I've never been in the bath and I never want to; it's made for a giant. Near the door on the floor are some weighing scales; ribbed black rubber, where two feet stand, are either side of a huge glass eyeball. I would never get on them; the eye might see me looking down at it if I wasn't careful.

Grandma is in the kitchen. I'm colouring my puzzle book with my crayons in the room at the front, the one with the sweets in the amber dish. The fire is laid with neat sticks on top of newspaper cubes that grandma folds. I've never seen her fold them, so I don't know that for certain; I imagine her doing it rather than grandpa.

I shall stop and go down the passage towards the kitchen; grandma might be getting tea ready.

As I pass down the passage, the larder door is ajar. Is it hard to push? I could see what it's like as I'm passing. I shall take this chance to feel its weight. I'm surprised to find it is very light and it moves without any effort.

Click. I know that noise well. My slight push and the door has shut.

"Fran, let me out."

Dumbstruck, with fear in my soul, I run as far away as I can. I hide behind the settee in the darkest corner of a room I rarely go in.

I stay with my fingers in my ears, without moving a muscle; rescue will arrive, I hope, sometime.

Hunger won't bring me out; neither the biscuits in the barrel nor the pretty wrapped sweets tempt me to move.

My already dark corner is becoming darker as night descends. All is very quiet. I feel sleepy.

I am scooped up by someone, at last, and taken up to bed.

B5 Formed Preferences

My mother has been in Maidstone Hospital a long time. On a few occasions, I have been collected from Bickley by my father and taken, along with my older sister, to visit her. Today is a visiting day.

It's a long way.

We turn and head up the long drive between some tall trees. The building now comes into view. I'm never aware of it as we drive through the gates, yet it is huge; it is well hidden behind a screen of trees. I don't go inside; my father goes in to announce his arrival while we sit on a park bench some way from the building.

Built of brick and stone, it has a mixed-up roofline. The building looms tall and dark. It's from a fairy tale but not a happy one. Happy fairy tales are those with cosy thatched cottages like I see on holiday.

My father returns to wait with us in the grounds. A few couples are out in the grounds walking together, but not many.

Eventually, I see my mother; she is striding towards us from the front entrance. These reunions don't give me any feeling of joy; I never feel excited while we travel here, as I do when we drive out to go on holiday.

My mother joins us; there's quiet chatting, she goes back in and we leave. I wonder what these visits are about. I could be back at Bickley, absorbed in a puzzle; I'd not have been upset if I had been told I was being left behind.

B6 Adult's Manipulation

It won't be long now before we will all be living back at Ash Close; we are going to Maidstone Hospital to pick up my mother.

I didn't like being sent to Bickley when my older sister was able to stay at home for the whole time.

The Maidstone Hospital would have been a worse place to be sent, though; it is so big and gloomy; from the outside, at least. I think it would be like that on the inside too; I'd have hated to go inside if I had been told to do so.

I hear nothing as to why my mother was there.

We are stopping on the way home for a picnic. I hope it will be somewhere like Keston Ponds.

Keston is a lovely place. In the winter, when the water has iced over thickly, my parents put on their skates and join all the other people gliding round.

Unsafe areas are sectioned off with roped posts. The ice is checked regularly for cracks when the water freezes.

Today it is warm; the sun shines. There'll be no ice.

Our stopping place has no ponds. Ordinary meadows surround us. My father pulls up the car and we all unload, ready to picnic behind the roadside hedge out of sight of the lane.

While packing up after the picnic, I sense an uneasiness. There's a clipped flurry of words between my parents.

Thankfully, it has stopped now that we have reached the car.

It was: "a storm in a teacup", as Granny is fond of saying at Windyridge.

We pile into the car to go home with the upset settled; my father is seated to drive home.

While I was staying at Bickley, my father said goodbye to the Austin 7. He now drives a Standard 8, which has more room in the back for the three of us.

This car isn't starting.

The Standard won't move. My father keeps trying, but the car won't spring into life. The battery is healthy. He tries again; he's muttering to himself, obviously concerned.

In the back, we sit in silence. Waiting.

Another quick exchange of words about who should be driving before my mother pulls a strange black object from her pocket.

She silently opens her door. They are changing places; the battle as to who should drive the car is over . . . won by my mother, it seems.

As soon as my father saw what she was holding, he went to swap places suddenly.

On her way around the front of the car, she lifts the bonnet then closes it, moving around to drive. My father is already across to be the passenger.

No words are spoken. The car starts first time. We travel in complete silence.

She knew all along that my father was not going to start the car.

Who should drive? I don't think my friends' families have such issues to sort out when they picnic. But neither would their mothers be removing part of the car to prevent it from moving, I think.

Such a tiny object.

My mother tells me it was the rotor arm she took from under the bonnet.

B7 Different World

I'm on my way to school. My mother walks with me. I have no feelings about it as I don't have any idea what will be involved during a day at school.

We walk through a stunning field of high, ripe, golden corn. I cannot see over it. Its stems are strong and grow straight up. The path trodden through allows just enough room for me to walk beside my mother. The path is bare of weeds; the soil is beaten flat by many feet, I guess.

I'm listening to the gentle rattling of the wheat heads as they rub shoulders in the breeze. I'm thinking about how the path got into the field because there's no sign that wheat ever grew on this long strip of bare soil stretching through the field. It feels like it was put here especially for me to walk to school today. No one else is here in the field using this cut-through. How did the corn know not to grow on the soil? If it had, we would not be able to pass through today. It is amazing and I want to walk through it again tomorrow.

The school stands alone, surrounded by fields. I can tell it's not old. The low, neat building is surrounded by a tidy brick wall built no higher than the corn in the field. The metal gates are wide and stand open; the broad path leads straight to the glass front doors. I'm wondering what I will find inside this pleasant-looking school.

I will soon find out what it is all about; I knew this day would come for me because all children start school when they are young.

While walking through the corn, up the path and through the doors into the school, we have seen no one. The field was empty, and now the school feels empty of people too.

My mother knows where to go as she heads straight to a door on the right leading off the entrance lobby. I feel she's been here before because she is very confident and doesn't need to find someone to direct her.

The big room is full of children. I can't make out what is going on. They are all moving about strangely like beings from another planet. This is school?

I turn to my mother for help. She's gone. The door is shut. I don't know what to do. I'm overwhelmed.

I cannot help but sob. My tears fall, and keep falling. I hear nobody, I see nobody. I can only stand and sob uncontrollably with my eyes shut tight. I want to be rescued from this strange world.

The teacher is playing the piano with her back to the class. She eventually rises and comes across the big room, towards me. She scoops me up and sits me on her knee at the piano.

With me on her knees between her arms, she continues to play and I continue to sob. Her arms move about as her hands dance up and down the piano keys and suddenly, with a booming voice, she calls out:

"Arms in the air!"

After more bouncing on her knee, her voice once again reverberates inside my tummy:

"Drop!"

I can't see the children, the many children. I only see the black and white notes and her quickly moving hands passing this way, then that, upon them. It's an alien world I'm in; I've no idea what it's all about.

I'm sitting on a lady's knee; I don't know what she looks like. I do know she has a booming voice, though. I can only sit and cry through what feels like an eternity.

I'm lifted down and told to find a bed to lie on.

A bed in school? But I don't feel like sleeping. I turn around to find each child lying stretched out in silence, on a collection of small beds. All are perfectly positioned as in a graveyard. All their feet are facing the same way.

I've stopped crying. Now I stare in dismay. What is this about? Where did the beds appear from? Why are the children pretending to be asleep?

The corn field this morning was a strange new experience; I liked it. School, too, is a new strange experience, but I definitely don't like it. Not one bit.

B8 Parent Roles

Our Standard 8 is black; most cars I spot are black.

My mother has been around cars all her life. Being shown how to work with tractors and cars was part of life in the farming community of her upbringing. She was never required to take a driving test to use the open roads, she tells me.

Cranking cars with the starting handle, topping up the radiator, changing batteries or wheels — none of these is an issue for my mother.

Her family car was a soft-topped Singer Tourer. By having the top down, standing room was provided, which was always useful. The Singer could then hold the big family.

There's no car at Windyridge now.

I've not seen any of my four aunts drive a car, neither aunty Josephine, aunty Jean, aunty Dulcie, nor aunty Sheila.

I've seen mother's sisters drive tractors sometimes, but never cars.

After she left Stonar School, my mother became a chauffeur within the Wingham community. Then she was recruited during the war to instruct ambulance drivers. She was in the ARP and gave her instruction under the orders of the BSM. She still has some of the large, shiny buttons from her uniform. Embossed with ARP in large letters, they are the biggest and finest in our tin of spare buttons.

She has more knowledge of cars than my father. It is she who is under the bonnet rather than he. Heated words about who is to drive are quite normal. I think it's because she likes to be in control at the wheel; it's not that he's a bad driver. I've never heard her complain about my father's driving.

Ashcroft is my aunty Milly's chauffeur. He drives her, with her son Richard and my great-aunt May, to visit us just for the day. He drops them off here in Ash Close and then returns to pick them up later. Ashcroft never comes into our house, not for lunch, not even for tea. He wears a dark blue uniform and a peaked cap similar to that of a train driver. He drives some hundred miles from Woking to Petts Wood and then back again, all on the same day.

Aunty Milly is my mother's cousin. Great-aunt May and my granny are sisters. They have many brothers and sisters.

B9 Communications Absent

I'm to be driven over to the farm where I go to fetch rabbit food. It won't be a route I know as we are travelling by road.

When I go on my fairy cycle, I go through gates, through woods, over a level crossing, and along tracks to reach the farm. I usually go to pick up corn or hay for my rabbit, Snowy.

I'm told to fetch her from her run.

Unusually, she is to come too. I hold her close. So warm and silky, her little nose twitching. I stroke her ears back, flat to her head. She likes that and doesn't struggle.

Snowy is spotted all over, black and white. She's an Old English rabbit. I don't think she loves me as much as I love her because she regularly burrows, trying to get under the chicken wire fence of her run, to escape. The wire had to be buried so that she's no longer able to get out.

Why the journey today? Why is Snowy coming too?

We arrive, and she's briefly taken away.

She's back home in her run, and I have more hay and food. What was it all about? Snowy was taken away by the farmer and soon handed back. Perhaps he was showing her to his wife because Snowy is a lovely rabbit.

I'm told she will have babies.

Oh, how exciting!

I'm checking every day now. Please, let it be today. I don't know what to expect. I think I will see tiny Snowies. Lots of them.

Nothing.

Nothing today, either.

Always nothing. The days keep passing; I keep looking.

I'm told it won't happen now, but I can't stop looking, hoping my parents are wrong.

I've not been driven to the farm again. I go on my cycle as usual. Snowy doesn't have babies.

I was given a farmyard on my last birthday. It was all carefully handmade except for the animals. It has pigs, cattle, sheep, horses, geese and chickens but no rabbits. I've decided to make some myself out of plasticine.

B10 Unexpected Relief

A hospital is never a place I think I might go. I'm too young.

I know I was born in Bromley Hospital and that my mother and her older sister were both nurses at Guys Hospital before they were married. My older sister had her tonsils and adenoids removed in one. My mother was in Maidstone Hospital for ages.

My father broke his little finger on his left hand while playing cricket just before we went to Dymchurch on our summer holiday. It was thickly plastered and looked very funny. That may have meant a visit for him, from his school in Erith.

Before the picnic today, my father drops us off at church. Going to church is our normal Sunday ritual, then the usual roast dinner cooked by mother at home. Today our lunch is to be a picnic.

Until now, I always thought that the car stayed put; that my father sat there in the driver's seat for an hour until we four came out of church. My image now has to change; my mother tells me that my father drives away and then comes back to pick us up.

"He's down the road reading the paper."

I picture him sitting in the driver's seat, opening the huge newspaper over the steering wheel — a very cramped place to read the big paper. This is a more amusing scene than the last I had in my head, of him just sitting waiting outside the church patiently. So he spends the hour with *The Times*?

The Times is important to my father:

"Don't do that! Your father doesn't like the paper being touched before he reads it."

My father sits relaxed in the armchair, turning the large, awkward pages of the pristine newspaper, causing them to rustle and pop. It sounds like the fire starting to catch under dry sticks in the grate. The new, untouched pages sound crisp and brittle at every movement.

After a page is turned with a rustle, there's a pause; then another turn, with a louder, quicker rustle. A longer pause, then two quick turns with a lot of crackle and pop, as if the fire is now well alight. Silence briefly, followed by a sudden flurry of turns; sometimes the pages are turned backwards very quickly.

Tea is being prepared in the kitchen; it's a long session of on-and-off paper noise for me, as I sit at the table drawing the tree in the garden, which I can see through the window.

Listening to the paper's noises behind me, I cannot make out a fixed pattern. I cannot guess what will come next, a long or short rustle or a very long crackle and pop.

My mother announces with confidence:

"Your father reads the paper twice over I think, just to annoy me."

After tea, my mother takes up her knitting. She's turning the heel of a sock; click click . . . click click click. Long pause. Click, pause, . . . click click click. Finding a pattern to this noise is also impossible. My mother looks down, now and then, to the arm of the chair; knitting instructions for the sock rest open on its flat surface.

My mother hates the newspaper noise. Perhaps my father hates the knitting needles clicking?

After returning from school, he comes through the front door, then picks up the untouched *Times* from the hall table and settles in his armchair. Rustle, crackle and pop till tea is on the table; this is his routine, and my mother's in the kitchen.

At the church, I run out at the end of the service. The car is there in the same place, just the same as last week; nothing has changed. But now I know it moves when I'm out of sight. My thinking that the car was standing there all the time I was in church was just an illusion. I feel rather shocked that what I thought took place place was not the truth; I could have believed it forever.

Off now to a picnic spot. Which one will it be? What delights will it hold?

Fields are crossed, with us each carrying different items. We reach a wide, slow-running stream. The stream has a little shore so I can leave my shoes close to the water; with bare feet the pebbles are hard to cross to reach the water, otherwise.

Venturing in, I'm looking for things in the water. Little fish perhaps, or sometimes I've even seen crayfish in streams; perhaps I will see some of those here. A large dragonfly catches my eye as it rises awkwardly from the rushes.

Peering back into the water, I see a red cloud at my feet. How strange it is. I move my feet to disperse it. The cloud is taken with the current, but it builds again quite quickly.

My foot? Lifting it up, I see blood dripping into the water. It's plopping fast from under my right foot.

I calmly hobble out of the stream. My younger sister calls as I leave the water:

"Where are you going?"

"I've cut my foot."

I'm crossing the grass on my heel; no shoes, as I don't want blood in those. I need it looked at, that's all.

As I lift my foot for a close inspection, the blood drips. It's my father who blurts out:

"Hospital case!"

I let out a sudden bawling like I've never bawled before. No! Not that place. The shock announcement is too much. My face turns white, with my heart beating as if it will explode in my chest.

All plans are suddenly changed. There's to be no picnic, no food; everything is hurriedly packed. A half-full green glass bottle is fetched from the stream, and we head for the hospital.

I'm a wreck, unable to adjust to my being taken to such a place.

The car is stopping but not outside a hospital; it's a doctor's house, I'm told.

I quickly recover; doctors are not terrifying.

As I seat myself for the doctor's inspection, I listen to this stranger's calm voice. I become interested: at no point have I felt pain, not even when the glass cut open my foot. The cut isn't visible to me, only to the doctor.

He tells me he is going to put three stitches in my foot to bring the cut closed. I'd like to watch, but the angle of my foot isn't allowing this. As I sit here on the seat, I cannot see him working on my foot, sadly.

I must walk on my heel now until the cut mends itself, he tells me. I show him how I can do it and promise I won't forget. He says oour own doctor will take out my stitches in ten days' time. It's a long time to hobble, I think.

The stitches are removed as the cut is healed. Our doctor tells my mother:

"She can now walk properly."

But I can't.

In my mind, the cut will split open. How does anyone know that won't happen? I don't want to risk it.

I hobble for weeks; no reassurance from anyone reduces my fear. Eventually, my mother takes me back to our doctor. I explain my fear.

He turns to my mother, saying he has the answer; I'm so impressed because once we get to our home, I remember his instruction to my mother; it has worked like magic:

"You will have to distract her."

B11 Feeling Vulnerable

Mostly we camp on farms when on our summer holidays. This holiday we are on a farm in Dorset near Corfe Castle. A real castle is a big attraction for my father, I think, as he teaches History. I much prefer sand castles.

We are near the sea. I'm not afraid of the water. I'm not very keen on my navy-blue hand knitted swimming costume; when it's wet it sags and tells me it would sooner be around my knees.

I love building castles with moats that get filled by the incoming tide. I'm given little paper flags to stick in the turrets.

As the waves eventually reach it, I watch the base of my building change shape as wave by wave it is swept away. The turrets might fall without a wave ever touching them.

The only bit I hate about the sea is if my father carries me out in his arms beyond where I think I can stand up on my own.

I'm enjoying trying to play catch in the shallow water. My father has brought a tennis ball with him.

"Butter fingers!"

My hands have clapped shut, in mid-air, as the ball lands in the water. I'm used to being called butter-fingers. It means I can't catch a ball.

I'm scooped up in fun by my father as he laughs at my efforts. I can't catch but it's still fun. We are all laughing.

He carries me out into deeper water; I'm grabbed by fear.

I scream and shout loudly. My arms and legs grip my father tightly. I can't control the terror inside my head. I'm no longer in control of my life. Being held above deep water is not a safe place to be.

My screams are those of distress, no longer the squeals of delight that I was making when I was in the shallow water playing games.

"Let me go. *Let me go!*"

Only with my father walking back towards the shore can I be pacified. I don't know why he does it. My reaction is always the same; there's never any change.

Those poor kittens are in my head. I know they died in the waterbutt. My mind can see a picture of that moment. They were left without help, ignored, never mentioned by anyone. It was as if they never existed.

The kittens were brought wrapped in cloth, wanting to be loved. I thought they had been brought to the Vicarage for safe keeping.

The truth jolted me. I see them in my imagination, dropping into the deep water. I stood wondering about the adults around me, all ignoring what had happened.

I have no trust in anyone's arms if they hold me over deep water. I cannot swim.

B12 Absorbed Distraction

There are small lean-to sheds attached to our garage. One of these at the side of the garage in the passage alongside the house has the door slightly ajar.

I want to look inside. Lying on a small, round, wooden table supported by its thick pedestal base, is a tool with a wheel and handle.

This special red-painted tool is just lying on the table on its own. It draws me to pick it up and discover what it can be.

I turn its handle; it moves with ease and I enjoy the soft rattling noise it creates. I notice by doing this, the sharp metal spike at the end spins. I stand it upright on the table and turn the handle; the end of the spike starts to burrow into the wood. It sinks in easily, making a perfectly beautiful hole.

I'm amazed by its effect.

In the peace and quiet of the little shed, having worked out what the tool can do, I create many holes in the table. Sawdust rises from the mahogany table as the spike digs deeper in. The ease is like a dream; I repeat it again and again.

Brushing the sawdust aside, the holes the tool has made stand out clearly.

They are wonderfully formed in every way. With the sawdust brushed off, each hole's depth takes on a delicate orange colour. Their depths are not dark like the surface of the table.

I enjoy the tool's skill. I drill one hole after another. My father is not on my mind.

I realise that my holes will be in full view as soon as the shed door is opened. I hear my granny's words:

"Your sins will find you out!"

Days go by with the holes still on my mind.

My father shows no interest in them or how they got into the table. I wait, but nothing is mentioned.

B13 Assailed Nostrils

I'm walking to the shops in Petts Wood with my mother.

We pass the Daylight Inn. It stands on an island surrounded by trees, paths and bushes.

Further on from the Daylight Inn are toyshop windows with little models of all kinds of things. They give me ideas for my doll's house and my farm yard. I never go inside and neither do I get given anything I see in the windows, but that isn't why I look; I look because the items interest me. The smaller the better as my thatched doll's house and farmyard aren't very big.

The fishmonger's, which my mother visits each Friday, has a display built out onto the pavement. It's a lot further away from our house than the Daylight Inn.

Fish big and small are laid out on the slope of the platform; some look nothing like the fish that I've seen in a stream or pond, nor even in a book. All shapes and colours, their scales gleaming brightly whatever the weather. It's a pattern of open, bulging eyes and mesmerising long whiskers; fish that smell of distant seas in all their glory.

The large, sloping, wooden shelf comes lower down at the front so I can see most of what is arranged on it.

My mother goes into the fishmonger's while I wait outside. I have plenty of time to gaze; some of the shellfish are like those I've seen on the beach during our camping holidays. I might see them poking out from the sand or caught in the seaweed left at high tide: blue-tinged mussels or white clams. The tide tries to drag them out to sea again.

I've found razor shells long and gleaming, beautifully smooth and polished, caught in the shifting sands so they stand up tall. Most of the shells in the sand are only half the shell, but the barnacles and limpets on the rocks are complete; they don't have two halves like all the other shells I see. They are tightly fixed on the rocks like many little wigwams;

Neither are the winkles in two parts; they look like snails.

Along from the fishmonger's display is a side passage; there is a terrible smell coming from that direction. I slowly work my way down the fish-stand until I can peek around the corner and look down the track between the buildings. It doesn't go far. I can see a huge pile of large empty shells, all of them white and shallow like dollies' soup dishes.

I guess the dreadful smell is coming from this pile of wonderful shells. What are they? I've not seen them on the beach and I don't see them displayed in the front, yet there are hundreds and hundreds piled high down along the side of the fishmonger's. It's a puzzle, the smell and the shells.

Here's Mother.

In her bag, she will have bright yellow smoked haddock for Sunday breakfast and cod that always goes with white parsley sauce. Kippers, too, flat and so strange to look at. I can't imagine how they manage to swim when they are out at sea.

I think I only ever eat haddock, cod, kippers and herrings; all the rest that I saw on the rack are strange to me. I don't think my mother ever buys them.

The cod is eaten at dinner time, never for breakfast. Pudding will be custard with prunes that have to be soaked through the night. I like to arrange my sucked stones along the edge of my bowl to see who I will marry:

"Tinker, tailor, soldier, sailor, rich man, poor man, beggar man, thief."

I love prunes, so I have to go back to tinker, tailor sometimes.

B14 Impressive Change

A big event is to happen at father's school in Erith. He and my mother will both be attending. Mother is to have a special new dress for the occasion.

Nothing is sewn on the sewing machine as it is when I need a new dress. A '"ball" has been mentioned.

The only idea I have for a "ball" is that of pictures in a story book, *Cinderella*. She arrives at the ball in her glass slippers.

I'm in awe and wonder to think that my mother and father have been invited to such a splendid occasion.

Quite a time has passed; it's not been talked about recently, so I think it must all be over. It's not in my head at all now; it's as if I dreamt that my parents were going to a ball.

We walk to Petts Wood this morning; it's Saturday. We pass the large cinema that stands alone surrounded by rough, open ground. It looks as if it doesn't really belong to the town.

At this time on a Saturday morning, there are always lots of excited children older than me waiting to be let in through the huge doors at the front of the cinema. We pass on the opposite side of the street.

The queue is not like an adults' queue, all waiting patiently in twos. When adults queue at the cinema they talk in low tones as if they are about to enter church for a funeral.

These children are bunched up together; there's no pushing but plenty of noisy, excited chatter. One day I will be old enough to join them to see what the excitement is all about. I must first grow quite a bit taller.

Back home after lunch, my mother 'pops out' for a long spell at the hairdresser's in town. Tonight is the "ball", she tells us!

With every hair on her head now in a special position, she moves around the house more carefully; it's as if she's received instructions to be a puppet. It's amusing to see how slowly she moves her head when she turns to talk. Maybe she believes a jerk might disturb her hair.

They aren't leaving till late when it will be dark and we will all be in bed. I hope we will see her in her ball gown. I've no picture of it in my head, only of Cinderella.

Father calls us from our beds, and we gather in the front room ready for my mother to come down the stairs and enter the room. I can't explain the expectation I have of what I am about to see. I am gripped with excitement, knowing but not knowing.

I gape in disbelief. This lady cannot be my mother!

Her long dress of peacock satin rustles as she enters. It hugs her waist before it reaches up onto her bodice; the bodice is jewelled, with many tiny gems sparkling to dazzle my eyes.

There are no straps on her shoulders! My mother's shoulders are bare; how does the dress stay up without straps, I wonder? I'm fascinated.

She looks magnificent. Beyond anyone's imagination, certainly beyond mine.

B15 Surprising Alert

It's cold enough to have the coke stove alight in the kitchen, along with the coal fire in the dining room. I more often than not see my mother rather than my father lighting the dining room fire. It's usually laid ready with crunched newspaper and small sticks that have been collected from the woods, then topped with carefully balanced pieces of coal.

If she has any difficulty in getting it going, my mother holds an open sheet of father's *Times* across the fireplace; the struggling fire is then hidden from my view. She saves an old newspaper just for this purpose.

I'm transfixed watching my mother holding it in place with both hands along the edges; it fills the open space perfectly. It is held vertically, arms stretched with the print not far from her face, as if she is struggling to read the news.

Reading is not on her mind; I've never seen my mother reading any newspaper, only knitting patterns and *The Lady*.

I watch the stretched-out sheet. Orange light is flickering from behind in the grate. Soon there's crackling and the orange light spreads across the whole area behind the paper. I feel the paper should be pulled away for fear of it catching alight, but my mother continues to grasp it confidently, just like I've seen my grandad do at Windyridge.

If a small patch of black appears, the paper is singeing; rarely does the singe grow large enough to catch the paper alight because the paper is removed at that point. It never looks like an action of great urgency; it's never considered an emergency, though it looks alarming to me.

Neither Grandad nor my mother ever needs to puff on a fire to get it going as long as they have *The Times* or another large sheet of newspaper handy.

It's been a peaceful day but cold enough for my mother to tong some glowing coals onto the coal-shovel to take them into the front-room so she can quickly develop a fire in that grate also. Both are stoked up to warm the whole house.

I feel comfortable knowing that the warmth will eventually reach inside me through my clothes. I'm tempted to rest my feet nearby so they can feel the fire's warmth.

"Feet away from the fire unless you want more chilblains!"

The warm peace is disturbed by a knock on the front door. It's a neighbour with news for my mother.

Chimney on fire?

How did he know? What did he see? All our fires look perfectly normal. I look at both and see neither has any flames, just glowing coals.

Everyone drops what they were doing. They head outside and stand looking up at our chimney. What are they looking at?

As I reach the open front door, the smell coming from outside is unpleasant. I reach the group in the road and glance up at our chimney.

"Wow!"

Going straight up into the sky, without any hint of a direction change, is a thick plume of black smoke. Steam engine smoke is not as black or as thick. Nor does steam engine smoke smell quite like this.

I stare at the wonderful orange embers that are being propelled out, up amongst the thick, black plume. It's a powerful sight, yet we were totally unaware of it until the knock came on our door.

Neighbours bring salt for the grates to extinguish the fires. The fire brigade has been called. Why are they coming now when the fires are out?

"The fire is high up inside the chimney stack."

"Why is it there? We didn't light a fire up there. It all sounds silly.

B16 Deceived Eyes

I'm looking out into the darkness. It's a chilly evening. We are piled onto the cold back seat of the car; I happen to be in the middle between my two sisters. We are heading out to visit friends of my parents for the evening; they live not too far away.

A little way down past the church, we turn right towards where my older sister's friend Sandra lives; then even further on is where my sister goes for her piano lessons. I too have a friend who lives along this road. I know this area well but I've never been to visit my friend's house, though she visits me to play quite often.

Few cars are ever about this late; the only light visible is from the windows of houses set some way back from the road and the beam of our car's headlights.

Our progress is steady but slow. My father is driving all five of us. We are closely packed together. Being positioned in the middle, I can just see between the shoulders of the two adults; I have a view of the road ahead as I'm perched on the edge of the seat with my arms resting between the front seats.

Something on the road sparkles in the beam of our car's headlight as we turn right. I see it for just a brief moment. I have no doubt in my mind as to what I saw in the road:

"Dad! Stop! It's a watch. I saw a watch on the road."

We have travelled on.

I'm assured it was not a watch. I'm sure they didn't see it otherwise they would know it was a watch.

"Please, please. It was a watch I saw."

Reluctantly my father turns the car and back we go. Nothing; no sparkle to be seen.

"Further back Dad. I saw it as we were turning the corner."

I'm confident that I will see it any moment now because this is how our light's beam was falling, when I saw it briefly.

"There!"

The car halts. The sparkle is evident to us all now. I'm delighted.

"It *is* a watch!"

Why are they still insisting it isn't?

"Get out then; go and see."

I squeeze past everyone, relieved that at last I'm let out to go and retrieve it safely.

As soon as I have it in my hand I will be able to show them.

Strangely, the thing I've picked up is not a watch; in the dark I can feel that now. I'm back in the car, holding it tightly.

My parents chime together:

"It's a cat's eye."

It's not a watch, I know that now. But it's not a cat's eye, either. That is silly talk.

This hard bit of rock I fetched from the road is not a lost watch after all. I really believed that it was.

What made me think that it was? In my mind, I didn't want it to get squashed by a car.

We soon reach my parents' destination; the people are expecting us.

B17 Curiosity Satisfied

Thomas is a lad my age whose garden backs onto our garden behind the fruit bushes. He sometimes climbs through the fence where an upright board in the fence will slide to create a gap. It's behind the blackcurrants. It's not something I tell my parents.

We have a large wooden shed where we can spend time. He enjoys books about secret clubs so our shed is like our club's meeting place; it's important not to let the secret out.

We talk about stamps, cigarette cards, smoking and birds' eggs. He has quite a few birds' eggs which he says he will show me. With Thomas coming to our shed, my younger sister and I have the one chance to see what boys' private parts look like and Thomas has the chance to see a girl's. He is an "only child".

All three of us are curious; we have chatted about it through the fence. Outside in the garden isn't the place to settle such curiosity; I know that much. Our large shed is the ideal place.

It's serious. We all want to see the difference; my parents don't welcome such questions, and now I know Thomas has parents who are the same.

I once asked my parents, "Why can't men love one another?" It was greeted with a stony silence. I find it puzzling because I love Snowy very much and would marry her if I could.

We are all happy once we've looked.

B18 Shattered Belief

My father is building a bonfire for Guy Fawkes night; it will be bigger than his garden bonfires, which are always sited lower down the garden, more out of sight than this one.

I rarely see flames in the garden bonfire, just smoke wafting upwards from the centre. The smell is not unpleasant, but the washing is rarely left on the line if my father is going to light a bonfire. Even the neighbours are told that a bonfire is about to be lit so that they too can take their washing off their lines.

There's no green vegetation being put on the one he is building now because flames are needed tonight. It is made up of sticks, broken-up wooden fruit boxes from the greengrocer's and old canes that usually keep the chrysanthemums and gladioli upright.

Once broken up, the fruit boxes are called "matchwood"; the boxes break up easily when Father stamps on them.

Larger wood is brought from the garage where it was stored to keep dry. The finished bonfire is the shape of a wigwam as all the longer wood is laid to meet high at the top on the outside; they are the last pieces to be added. Our old clothes prop has been broken up and stacked around the fire.

My father fetched a new clothes prop recently when we were out in the woods; my parents were collecting bags of leaf mould for the garden.

I know from last year that this bonfire will have very little smoke and that it will crackle loudly when it is first lit. Before the match is struck, it is sprinkled with liquid from a large tin-can kept in the garage. It will help all the wood to catch quickly.

Tomorrow, on the 5th of November, we will hear, in the still darkness of the night, the popping sound of rockets exploding high above; and see the sky filled with pretty clusters of tiny coloured stars.

Many rockets will be set off in the gardens of the neighbourhood. Families spend weeks putting their firework collection together and making guys that are, until the night of the 5th, slumped at front gates for others to view in passing. We've never put a guy by our gate; I don't know why not.

We will be carefully handed a lit sparkler and be allowed to run around the garden and even the house, waving it until the sparkle creeps lower and lower down the stick, slowly becoming weaker. It will die out, leaving just a small glow where it was last sparkling.

All the guys, with their drooped heads, slumped against the hedges or walls by the pavement, will soon be carried through to be put atop the unlit fires.

Then to just wait.

The following morning, I will go searching the garden for spent rockets with their long wooden sticks and coloured tube-like tops. Last year I managed to find a big one. It hadn't been one of ours.

B19 Deprived Lads

When my parents are talking at breakfast this morning, their chat has a tone of concern. It's about boxes of fireworks and something that happened.

There are always talks given at school before Guy Fawkes to warn children about the dangers of fireworks. The worries aren't so much to do with the many bonfires but the fireworks themselves, which we are never allowed to touch or even see before they are lit by my father on the night. They are kept safe somewhere, away from us.

Breakfast is finished.

Our coats are being handed out quietly, along with scarves and gloves. Where are we going?

It seems we are to make a rare visit to a house in the Close. This neighbour's house is in the "'lollipop" of the Close, so we are not going far.

We are to view a "catastrophe". Our whole family troop over to the front door of the house. My father knocks.

We are greeted and directed straight into the front sitting room. The neighbours leave us once we enter. I am speechless; my older sister isn't:

"Crikey!"

What a sight greets me as I go into the room! No wonder they haven't come with us. It must be so awful for them to see their room unrecognisable like this.

Everything in the room is black: the walls, the ceiling, all the shelves, the furniture, together with even the smallest items on the shelves.

It's hard to make out particular things as there is no colour, and not much light falls on any of the objects.

I stare in dismay; in silence.

The long, low, flat boxes on the large table in the centre of the room are pointed out to me. I hadn't been looking at them. They, too, are black, looking much like a strange table covering; they cover much of the table's surface.

"That's where the family's fireworks were, in those boxes."

What happened here? Nobody is saying, so I can only guess.

So their two boys will have no fireworks for tonight?

B20 Magic Delight

Tomorrow is my birthday.

A few days ago, my father had his birthday. I don't like mine being when it is, but my father's is far worse; his is on Christmas Day! I don't ever expect to have a party on my birthday; I get invited to birthday parties but I never have one to invite them to.

Birthdays that come around at the end of December get lost in the excitement of the Christmas festivities and the coming New Year.

My thoughts on Christmas Eve are not about my father's birthday next morning; they are about going to bed before my usual time so as to wake up early to discover what's causing the bulges and points in my filled Christmas stocking. It is slipped in when I'm asleep and hung on the bottom post of my bed by my mother or my father.

I try to stay awake to hear them coming in but I never succeed. I would never let on if I were to manage it.

The stocking, I always trust, will be one of my mother's "30 denier". I'm very glad my Christmas stocking is always one of my mother's most stretchy, thick, strong ones. She wears this warm type in the winter.

A sheer silk stocking that my mother wears in the summer would hold very few things. Spiky corners would make holes in the silk and shoot big ladders up the stocking. A bulging, laddered stocking would not be pleasant to wake up to.

My stockings are filled with many exciting things, none of which are wrapped.

My thoughts are never on my father's birthday, more on the little white sugar mouse I always look forward to finding, with its string tail and pink, bulging eyes. I never eat my mouse. I keep him here on my bedside table.

We all go to bed knowing when it is our birthday the next morning, but I don't know whether others will remember mine. When morning arrives, I will have my answer.

To wake up and find something new sitting on my bedside table is a most wonderful feeling. However small it is, the item being there when I wake means my birthday has been remembered.

I am always thrilled by this first sign.

On waking today, I see my birthday has been remembered!

Sitting on my bedside table is a glass globe like a fortune teller might wrap her hands around before she peers in to see a fortune, maybe.

Now that I'm sitting up in bed, I'm able to see inside the glass dome. There's a model castle; so sweet and highly detailed with turrets and battlements, and a perfect grass hill on which it all stands.

I smile to see it trapped within the glass, not unlike the ships I've seen within bottles. They lie on their sides in shop windows at the seaside. I always want to stay longer to see the little ships up closer. They would not be given to anybody to be played with, and neither is my castle, I think.

I pick it up to look closer at its tiny portcullis.

I'm pleasantly surprised to see my castle's tiny world is gently snowing. I watch with delight. Where did it come from? How does it work?

It feels like the best present I've ever had. Unexpected magic. I love it!

B21 Anticipating Reception

The toboggan is brought down off the wall inside the garage where it hangs out of the way until it is required.

Snow has fallen quite thickly, so we are getting dressed up warmly. My liberty bodice is buttoned securely and woolly jumpers pulled over. Boots are warmed by the fire. We are going to some fields my mother knows. There it will be quiet enough to slide down the slopes as often as we like without interruption from other tobogganers.

The toboggan sits aloft on the car's roof, tied securely to the rack. We've had the toboggan ever since I can remember. It's well made, with shaped wood sloping up to form slides. Curving up at the front, it shows the two important metal runners as it hangs high up in the garage waiting for snow to fall.

My father will not be with us, so there will be room in the car to take my older sister's friend, Sandra. We will pass her house on the way.

Snow is no longer falling. The day is cold but bright. The hill beckons.

With two sitting astride the sledge, it moves well. All four feet are raised high in front so as not to skim the fresh snow, slowing us down. A rope is fixed onto the front for pulling the toboggan back up the hill. It's exciting to be out here; as expected, we are alone using this hill. My mother's choice was a good one.

It's hard work going back up the hill, not because of the weight of the toboggan, which moves very easily, but from picking my feet up from the deep snow. With every step, there's a distinctive crunch. The feel and the sound made in the snow by my steps are hard to describe because I don't know another sound like it.

I'm tired and happy after all the fun we've had; I'm happy to let my older sister and Sandra have the toboggan all to themselves.

Legs astride, they now seem to speed faster and further than any of us did before. It's like they are first in a race, soon to be announced the winners.

I'm watching in silence, as is my mother. They will reach a barbed-wire fence if they don't stop soon.

Too late. In seconds, they reached the fence; it happened so fast. Their speed took us all by surprise.

Mother is already down to untangle the two girls from the wire. Blood from Sandra's face drips onto the dazzling white snow. She was in the front; her face is gashed at length across the top of her right cheek.

Both girls are silenced by shock, as I am. No tears or noise, just a snowy silence.

It's a sobering experience.

The journey to deliver Sandra back home is also done in silence; all words have left us, it seems.

There are just thoughts in my mind now, concerning the delivery of Sandra to her mother. I'm glad that I'm told to remain in the car when we get there. I'm out of sight and out of earshot. I want to believe it didn't happen.

B22 Night-time Disturbance

It's night time; I've already been to sleep. I've woken to hear my parents shouting downstairs. What's going on?

I creep out of bed to reach the top of the stairs to see what's happening.

I've got far enough down the stairs, quietly, to be able to peep through the uprights of the bannisters. I have a full view of them both as I look down.

Neither of them knows I am here, even though I am near them. They are beneath me in the passage; my father's back is against the closed kitchen door. They are at a dead end as the door to dining room is also shut. My father is pinned there by my mother. It's an intense row that I'm witnessing.

The way my mother's right knee is being lifted up sharply in front of my father tells me she wishes to do harm. She is aggressive, and I am shocked by her vehemence.

Two adults shouting in the night, then my being woken by it, is very disturbing. It happens at Windyridge sometimes when aunty Jean is not well. It's usually because she's not taken her medication.

My aunty has long spells in an asylum. Chartham is where she usually goes.

My mother spent quite a while away, quite recently; that was a hospital in Maidstone. I've heard that it, too, was an asylum; I eavesdropped on the adults talking about it.

People that get married love one another, or so I was led to believe in stories. But this is not true. I know my parents do not love one another; I wish they did. It's easy to tell if people love one another.

Their eyes are locked. They are in the light of the passage, still unaware that I am above them, crunched up on the stairs. There is no glance up.

I must creep back up and slowly climb back into be; I'd hate them to see me.

With my heart racing, I lie thinking, until eventually I fall asleep again.

I wake up in the night to find my sheet under me is wet; I wet the bed yet I don't recall it at all. The wetness is icy cold and uncomfortable, so I don't want to stay in bed.

Even though I know my bed is where I should be, I take myself into my parents' room, carefully climbing up and over to squeeze down between them. Only then do I know I shall be able to fall asleep again, dry and warm.

I go into my parents' bed a lot now in the night if I wake, even though my bed is dry.

Recently my mother has slipped a dark navy sleeve over my right thumb. It's tied around my wrist so that I can't take it off. It's been put on my hand to stop me chewing my right thumb knuckle which has now developed quite an unnatural-looking bulge. My skin has become tough in the place I chew, so it never minds me doing it; it doesn't hurt to have my teeth attack it. It never bleeds.

I know people bite their nails; much older people, too. But I don't do that; I chew my right thumb joint instead.

B23 Achieving Authenticity

I don't want to go to school. I'm lying in bed thinking about how I can manage to stay at home in the morning.

I can't say that it's to do with school because it's not. That would not be true, if I said school was the reason. It might cause my parents to turn up there; I'd hate that to happen.

So I can't make something up as that could lead me into trouble.

I've heard people talk about having a headache. They complain when they have one or even when they might get one, ...

"Stop it, you'll give me a headache."

It's not something anyone can see, so it's hard to imagine what it would feel like to have one. I've never had a headache, but if I had one, it would mean I could stay at home in the morning.

My bed is always close to the wall, so I will see whether banging my head on the wall several times will give me a headache. I believe it might.

If ever I've hit my head by accident, I've never had a headache from it. I will have to bang it quite a few times to get it to work, I think.

I hope no one hears me as I don't know what I would say if they discover it's what I'm doing.

I manage three or four times. It's not working. It's harder work than I thought to get myself a real headache.

My mother and father might be more friendly towards each other in the morning, even though they never appear to love each other.

I shall go to sleep now. In the morning I will think about it again.

B24 Family Gathering

There is a lot of talk about the Queen getting crowned. I'm looking forward to seeing the golden coach pulled by horses like in a fairy tale.

We are all going over to Bickley to watch the Coronation on grandpa's television. Grandma will get tea ready for us in the back room. Everything will be just the same as the last time we were there, except the television will be on.

The Union Jack is very difficult to draw; I've been practising it at school. Mother thinks grandma will have their big old flag flying from the white pole above the front door. I've never seen any flag flying there before. It's because this is a special occasion, a "very rare event".

The flag is always draped over the blanket chest at the top of the stairs. It's old and faded; it will look better hanging from the pole than it does covering the chest, though.

If I were brave enough to lift the corner of the flag I could peek inside. I expect it is full of woolly blankets stored for the winter. Before my eyes would see anything I would guess it was something woolly from my immediately smelling the moth-balls wrapped inside the blankets. I've never liked that smell.

I can't think of anything I like at Bickley. At home, I like the tea set aunty Pixie gave my mother for a wedding present; it has tiny flowers all over it. There would be no room to put any more flowers. Every space is covered except for the inside where the tea goes, and the handle, which is the same soft, greeny yellow. I also like the dinner plates we have; they have crocuses painted at the edge. The crocuses are bold and very colourful.

There are no animals or other children to play with at Bickley. It's a boring place to be.

I hope I'm not told to sit up at the table for teatime before I have a chance to see the horses pulling the golden coach. That's the bit I'm looking forward to most.

B25 Interior Revealed

I'm told to put on my best clothes today.

My mother is going to the Daylight Inn in Petts Wood and she is taking me with her. The walk is a short distance through the builder's yard.

To be visiting an Inn!

I've never been inside an Inn.

The Daylight Inn looks like it will be very light inside. There are windows all over the building; each window has many small glass diamond panes. It reminds me of the model my sister brought home that she made at school: an Elizabethan house with black-painted timbers between its windows. This building has plenty of real black beams criss-crossing between its windows.

Sometimes, when we are out in the car, my parents stop outside an Inn. We three sisters stay in the car while my mother and father go in. We are never allowed to get out of the car.

To be free to go inside this Inn, in the middle of Petts Wood, is quite something. What is in an Inn?

My mother leads me into a large hall with the light streaming in through the windows. There is a high stage with long blue velvet curtains pulled to the sides; on it, in the centre, stands a polished, black grand piano, gleaming like our much smaller upright piano. In front of the piano keys is a stool like the one at home, with a lifting padded seat; sheets of music are kept inside our piano stool. The piano stool at Windyridge is round and padded; it spins round and round to alter its height. It has no space for sheet music.

There are few people sitting in the big hall; plenty of rows of chairs, though. The audience is dotted around in small groups. My father isn't here; my mother has brought just me.

Any talking has now become a muffled murmur as a single small girl walks in from the side of the stage towards the piano. She's not looking at us.

One after the other, children come onto the stage, alone, to play a short tune. I don't know any of the tunes or the children.

I'm very surprised and quite alarmed to see, who I think is my older sister walking on. In her best frock, which I recognised straightaway, she's sprung out from nowhere, as if by magic.

If I had walked on like her, I would have worn my apple-green taffeta dress gathered at the waist, with its broad white sash tied with a big bow at the back. It was made especially for me to wear at a wedding. I don't remember whose, but I love the bridesmaid dress they gave me.

My sister plays a tune I've heard her play at home. The scattered groups of people around the hall clap. The claps are swallowed up into the high, elaborate ceiling hung with chandeliers.

When all the children have played a tune, the audience makes a move towards the front entrance of the Inn and that is that; my older sister has vanished along with all the others that came and sat at the piano, played and walked off again.

So an Inn is a big hall with a stage, a piano and lots of chairs?

B26 Displayed Disapproval

Things are packed for the weekend. We are driving to Reading where we will be staying at Reading School. Peter is a housemaster of the boarding school, so he and his family live on the premises.

The large bay window of their sitting room is to the left of the very impressive front entrance of the old, established school building. The window looks across the playing fields where cricket is played. The grounds stretch way down to a row of planted trees on the roadside along the frontage of the school grounds. They are very large as they were planted a long time ago.

It's always an amazing place for me to visit. Peter and Joyce have two boys quite a bit older than me. We children always have the run of the school grounds in the school holidays; complete freedom.

The boys have a hand cart. Many narrow paths link the low, outer-lying school buildings. They are happy to pull me along, with lots of fun and laughter. They closely miss the carefully planted flowers along the paths' edges as they screech the cart around the corners.

The wheelbarrow is a fun transport; they land me in the flowers as it tips over. I try to stay balanced by gripping the sides of the barrow firmly, but it's hard to keep hold. Both boys appear totally surprised when their load is hurtled into the marigolds. I join in their harmless fun with enthusiastic hilarity.

We are called in for tea and then free again till bedtime. The bedrooms we five children use are far from the adults' rooms, in another wing, which makes it feel as if we have the whole of the old school building to ourselves.

My mother has made an appearance before we are up and out this morning. She is visibly shocked to find us all sitting cross-legged together on my bed.

It's later; she's speaking to me about it while I'm alone.

We were having a good discussion about comics. The bed was the obvious place to sit in the absence of other furniture. I thought it was a sensible place to sit and chat; my mother did not.

We all use the school's indoor swimming pool. I still can't swim, so I'm given an inflated rubber ring for around my waist. The boys chase each other and jump high up and into the pool to avoid being caught. Water goes everywhere. They go right down out of sight in the water, but then they are soon up again like a cork. I wonder how they do that; it's so interesting to watch.

Another schoolmaster has a baby; it's not yet walking. In the water with his parents, the baby is enjoying it just as much as Peter's boys. The baby has nothing to help it float when the parents let it go. I stare in utter amazement as it bounces around on top of the water on its own!

They all come to swim here regularly. I don't go in water often, except when on holidays near the seaside, so I don't feel that comfortable. I wish I was like them; they all look so free of any concern. All are laughing and happy.

This is a great place in the winter too, because the swimming pool is heated. We can use it in the coldest weather.

A new baby in a big new pram has been brought round to be shown off to Peter and Joyce. The pram's shining wheels are bigger than those on the boys' bikes. We are all having teatime together in the grounds by the back door. I've never been aware of a baby this small before up close; I can't keep my eyes off it. I wasn't too interested when my younger sister was this young.

If ever I get given a doll of my own, I will call it Alison, just like this baby.

Peter has an operatic voice. When we visit, we usually go to hear him sing at the local theatre. Tonight it is *The Mikado*.

On our last visit, we heard him sing the lead in *HMS Pinafore*. The Company seems to sing a lot of Gilbert and Sullivan. It will be a busy late night, with lots of people getting settled in their seats before the curtains glide back.

The audience has hushed. The bright colours of the costumes and the scenery always take me by surprise, even though I'm already expecting them. The lights are brighter and the voices louder this time, it feels.

Today is the day we are to return home. I'm going towards the dining room for breakfast; Peter suddenly bursts into song. His deep voice echoes around the corridors. The powerful sound always takes me by surprise, enough to give me shivers from my head to my toes. It's terrifically exciting and seems to reverberate throughout my whole body like that of a ship's fog horn, especially when he's near me.

Now we have been waved off goodbye from the large front door of the old school. I can't wait to come back here and once again be driving slowly up between the trees of this long drive. The feeling in my tummy when arriving up this drive is one of total joy.

B27 Parental Misjudgement

There's one friend who is able to walk around to my house as hers is not far from Ash Close; she comes quite often to visit. I've never visited her house.

My friend is to visit this afternoon. It's not a good day for being outside, so I shall think of something to do inside. There's only ever her and me; it's always good times in or out, we don't mind which.

Painting, making models out of odds and ends, French-knitting; we have lots of choice inside. While busily occupied, we chat undisturbed.

I shall suggest we sit opposite each other at the dining room table and do our portraits. We've not done it before.

She likes the idea, so we settle down with our paper and crayons. We are happy to be left alone; nobody ever needs to enter the room when we are busy.

Finished, we pack all the stuff away.

At the front door she turns, waves goodbye and heads home, her picture I drew in her hand; I have hers of me, in mine.

Back in the room at the table, I get absorbed further, this time going through my stamps. My Godmother has given me some stamps she found for me when she was in New Zealand. I know I won't have them already and there'll be lots of space on the page set aside for New Zealand. Some pages, such as British Columbia, are completely empty.

I hear a knock on the front door; my father, I guess, will go. He's reading *The Times* in the front room.

I hear shouts at the front door. Two men shouting. I can make out that one is my father. I don't know the other voice. Is it a neighbour? What has caused such an upset? I'm curious but I have little real interest, even to think I might like to find out later. I'm quickly back into sorting my exotic stamps of birds and flowers as some, I realise, are from other islands near New Zealand.

It's now quiet again. I hear the front door shut loudly, a sign that my father is still very angry.

Now my door is flying open, shattering my peace. My father, red-faced with rage, directs his gaze straight at me. I'm in shock, mystified and terrified at the same moment. It's like nothing I've ever heard before. What is it about? What is going to happen?

Why were two men angry, and now why is my father standing here shouting at me?

"It was the worst thing you could ever do to your friend. Whose idea was it?"

I feel drained; I can hardly speak. I realise it was my friend's father who had been shouting at the door. It was about our portraits, then!

I struggle to even whisper the word:

"Mine."

That is the moment I'm condemned. I'm not hearing what my father is shouting at me.

I'm silent with my own thoughts:

I'm not "malicious" or "cruel". We were both happy doing our drawings. My friend was happy with her drawing as I was happy with mine . . .

My sin? I had dared to draw in her glasses.

They were on her face and I liked the pattern they made, that was all.

I know my friend is gone. She will not be visiting my house again. I don't think my friend and I see things as our fathers do. Nothing we were doing upset us, but both fathers became furious with me.

B28 Placebo Effect?

For some reason, my heels hurt when I'm walking. They don't hurt when I'm sitting down or lying in bed; they only hurt when I press on them, like on the ground when I walk.

I can't forget about my feet when I walk. The pain always comes.

I've mentioned it enough times now for my mother to decide to take me to the doctor's.

I've already guessed that he won't see anything, but the feeling is real. It's not like a splinter or a blister. Anyone can see those when they happen; this pain is different. There is pain inside the heels; they both have the same feeling when I step back onto them from my toes, yet there is nothing to see. I find this very strange.

The doctor studies my feet and announces to my mother:

"It's growing pains."

If that is what it is, I'm very glad it's only my heels that are the problem. Imagine if all your body had "growing pains". That would be terrible. I'm glad I only feel the discomfort when l put my heels on the ground.

The doctor tells my mother to rub on a special cream which he hands her.

I'm a bit surprised that the cream in the tub is so thick and dark. I was imagining something like calamine lotion, in a glass bottle.

This grim-looking stuff is rubbed on my heels before bedtime; there's no mistaking it once it is on, but my heels still feel the same in the morning.

My older sister has recently had her ears inspected for wax. Her having earache has caused her not to feel well.

A long time ago she used to get tonsillitis often which led to her going to hospital to have her tonsils and adenoids out. This meant that while she was in hospital she ate a lot of ice cream.

My mother had told her this before she went into the hospital so that she would want to go, I think. I'm not keen on ice cream so it would not have worked with me.

An ice cream van is often outside the school gates when we leave. Children queue to buy ice cream with their pocket money. I would never waste my money on it. I'm more happy with a packet of the wafers; they only cost a penny-ha'penny.

The thin glass thermometer which goes under our tongue when we are sick has broken. The mercury from inside the tube has escaped onto the table in many little shiny beads. As I guide them together, they join up to make bigger beads, but I cannot see a join, however hard I look.

I find I can easily poke the large ball of mercury to split it up again into a collection of lots of tiny, perfectly formed beads. I can make as many as I like by dividing them.

Few things are as fascinating as mercury; it behaves in such an unusual way.

It isn't possible to mend the thermometer, so a new one is to be bought tomorrow. I was lucky to have the chance to touch mercury, to know for myself how it reacts.

B29 Table Surprise

Downstairs, I'm excited to find a large, long box on the kitchen table. I guess it's arrived for me in the post; it's done up in brown paper and string. I have a close look at its stamps; l may want them for my stamp album.

On the morning of my last two birthdays, I've come downstairs to find a surprise on the kitchen table.

One year it was a farmyard with fields, trees, hedges and a yard. Also pigs, cows, horses and even carts and a tractor. I've since modelled my own rabbits out of warmed wax and made matchstick jumps for the ponies.

On my birthday before that, there was a doll's house on the table. It has a thatched roof made with real straw and little curtains at the windows. The front of the house can be unlatched and lifted aside so that I can add more furniture to the inside rooms and decorate the walls with tiny pictures.

Unlike those previous birthday presents, this one is wrapped up; I now have the extra joy of unwrapping it!

The parcel has arrived from Marlborough where my aunty Sheila now lives. She left the Vicarage in Wallingford because uncle John ran off with the district nurse. I don't know if he is still the vicar, but it's talked about with great surprise that a vicar should do such a thing. We've not visited my aunty in Marlborough yet.

The parcel isn't heavy. I soon cut the string from the red sealing wax and remove the paper. The lid of the box is as big as the box itself, as it slides down and hugs the box sides; I'm thrilled to see the label on the top of the lid; it reads in big, red letters: Puppet.

I carefully work the lid up, keeping it level as it fits so snuggly.

Laid inside the box is a puppet with its strings attached to two wooden slats that spread open to form a cross.

The head is made of a solid wooden ball with a green pointed hat instead of hair; it has a bright-eyed, happy face painted on. Moving joints are controlled by strings.

The flexible elbows, knees, shoulders and hips can't be seen as the shirt and trousers of the little chappy hide them all.

I wonder if aunty Sheila has been told that I love the stringed puppet on the television, in Muffin the Mule. I've never asked anyone for a puppet on strings because I never knew they could be bought in shops. I've never seen them there.

I have Sooty, but Sooty is a glove puppet that fits over my hand with my thumb and a finger moving his arms. My choice back then was to have Sooty rather than Sweep. Some of my friends have both Sooty and Sweep!

I shall practise hard with the strings of my new puppet so that it can walk along beside me. It's a wonderful present, such unexpected fun.

On the box, it reads 'Pelham Puppet'.

B30 Puppet Logistics

The stringed puppet aunty Sheila sent me is made of lots of pieces of bamboo. Most are similar in length. I can feel through the clothing of the puppet; they are all held together with string.

My father has similar sticks of bamboo holding up plants in the garden. Some are far taller than my father; he calls them "beansticks".

I never knew, before getting this puppet, that bamboo has a hole through it, big enough to thread a string.

I would like a stringed princess puppet, so I've decided to make one.

I have used papier mâché many times to make small bowls; once I made a hollow head for a glove puppet. That head had to be hollow so that I could nod or shake the head with my finger, but for a string puppet, it would only need space for the string to go up through to the hand-held crosspiece. I think it will be an easier head to make.

With plenty of newspaper and some flour to add to the final mix, I set to work. I've decided to wrap the papier mâché around the string to form the legs and arms, with a break along the papier mâché to form the moving joints of the elbows and knees.

I will leave enough string to attach solid feet and hands, modelled with a string coming out of the wrist and ankles to tie them on.

I'll work out how to do the body later. I shall have to decide whether it should have a break at the waist or not.

I lay all my pieces out to dry. Painting the limb sections pink when they are dry will mean a long wait, I expect. I've bulged the limbs so they are not straight sticks like the bamboo as my princess can then have bare arms. I imagine her in a net dress with lots of layers, rather like a ballet dancer in *Swan Lake*. Her dress will be long, though, and she will wear a tiara.

Tying all the pieces together is an exciting process. The limbs and head are now already painted.

I must consider her dress and tiara before I attach the longer strings.

What a moment that will be! It's been well worth the wait to reach this moment.

Receiving the unexpected Pelham Puppet was amazing; this feels a different excitement. I've made this excitement all on my own, with no help from anyone.

B31 Unenvied Lessons

I am to start piano lessons. I will have the same teacher as my sister and I will get taken to the same house. Will I be told, one day, to go on the Daylight Inn stage like she did?

My heart had beaten rapidly when I realised it was her on the stage. It felt as though it was me having to sit there and play. Never do I want to do what she did; never. Not even if I was to have the chance to wear my favourite dress.

I will wear my dress to a birthday party instead.

B32 Assistance Required

I'm in such a muddle. Strings everywhere. Where should they go? How long should they be? It's turning into an unfathomable "cat's cradle".

My princess is far from coming to life as I imagined. I need extra hands or perhaps an adult's help to sort out where the strings need to tie onto my cross piece of thick card that I will use to control her.

I've made plenty of holes, so there's no shortage of choice for tying the strings. The length of each string is very important as I want both her arms to be by her sides when she stands upright.

Attaching the strings to the crosspiece is the most difficult part of making a string puppet, I've decided.

Doing the dress was easy because her dress is not intended to ever come off. I glue her silver-paper tiara on with Gripfix.

This pot of sweet-smelling, white, waxy paste is very sticky. It is a clever paste; it never crinkles any paper when it is spread on.

I don't think the tiara will come off now.

My mother agrees to hold my cardboard cross up level with my waist so that I can thread through the strings one by one and finally get my puppet to come alive.

I'm very happy seeing my puppet successfully walking on her tip-toes. I shall give her ballet lessons now.

My older sister goes to ballet school in Petts Wood, but it's not something I want to do.

B33 Unforeseen Shock

News has arrived. It's to tell my mother that her favourite older sister Josephine, has died unexpectedly. She lived on a farm with uncle Roger and my two cousins, who are both a little bit older than my older sister.

Their farm is in Dumfries, Scotland. We meet up with them sometimes at my granny's down in Wingham. I only remember meeting uncle Roger once. He doesn't stay with us when our families are down at Windyridge, much like my father, who has his school work to do. Uncle Roger tends to the farm.

Our house is unusually quiet. None of us has been told to be this silent, we just are; this sad occasion has caused a hush to fall on the household.

When aunty Pixie was staying, we were asked to keep quiet as she was in bed upstairs, unwell. Aunty Pixie, my Godmother, was my mother's best friend when they were at Stonar School together.

Aunty Pixie had no living parents, so she spent a lot of time at Windyridge with mother and her three sisters, Josephine, Jean and Dulcie.

This feels different; there is no need to tell us how we should behave. There is a heavy feeling in our house that is hard to describe.

We usually all have Sunday breakfast at the table together, but this Sunday I get up early with my older sister to prepare and take our parents their breakfast in bed.

I have to watch the toast under the gas flames. I'm the right height to see it turning brown; I need to pull out the pan quickly before it burns. I turn it over to brown its other side. It's an important job that I like doing well.

I will also be allowed to carry one of the trays upstairs into the bedroom.

There are two big trays kept for breakfast in bed. Each has its own little dishes, one for the butter and the other for the marmalade. There are small china teapots too, both with matching milk jugs.

Laid out on the delicate white tray cloths, they look perfect, fit for the Queen, as Granny would say.

I hope my mother will get a piece of tea leaf stalk floating in her teacup when she pours hers. When she sees we have one in our cup, she says it's a sign that a friend is going to visit. I always find it a nice thought when I find one in my cup.

When she comes down to find everything put away tidily, I look forward to her saying:

"Oh, the fairies must have been!"

I hope she doesn't forget.

Few words are spoken now, but we still have teatime around the table and have our bath before bedtime as it's Sunday. I haven't experienced a death in the family before, to observe how it affects everyone.

B34 Woodland Discomfort

Once through the shortcut of the builder's yard and the town's streets are reached, the railway bridge soon comes into sight.

At night, from my bedroom window, I can hear the goods trains shunting across the bridge. It isn't a sound I particularly like. It's a night-time noise which I have grown to accept will be heard often when I lie in bed. The widows are open, so the noise is very clear on still nights.

I prefer the sound of the lawnmower when it is pushed, whirling with its blades clattering over the grass. The clippings collect in an attached metal box; there's always a pause when the mower is halted for the box to be emptied of cuttings further down the garden.

The smell of newly cut grass wafts up through my bedroom window. I lie and listen for the next pause in the clattering. This is when the sound of the swifts happily squealing overhead can be heard.

My two older cousins are staying. The shorter cousin has a mop of red hair and numerous freckles.

Confident and outgoing, she is taking off to the park; I'm happy to go too.

I shall wear my new slip-on shoes; these shoes were bought at Clarks in Bromley where we went to also buy smart shoes for my older sister. She is to attend a new school at the end of the summer holidays. I even had the chance to stand up with my feet inside the new x-ray machine; I could see the layout of the bones inside my feet!

The swings, roundabout and see-saw beckon first, followed by my thinking about the joy of the adjoining woods. All this wonderful space lies beyond the railway bridge.

I would never go alone as it's far off, so I jump at the opportunity to go with my cousin.

We play on the swings and the see-saw, then skip down the wide, beaten path to explore the woods. I know them well, but they are new to her.

She's a bit of a tomboy with an adventurous spirit, and I feel she, too, will love the woods — maybe more than the swings. Once further on into the trees, there are lots of smaller paths to explore; both of us are in a carefree, happy mood.

We see nobody about. We have the woods to ourselves.

The area is composed of native trees, with plenty of light filtering down through the large, spreading canopy. These woods are a splendid place to spend our time.

We reach a large clearing. The thick carpet of beech mast littering the floor attracts my attention.

I stand up suddenly from being crouched down, alerted by a shout.

My heart is now beating fast; we are surrounded by youths in what, to me, is dark, menacing attire. Some dozen or so. I feel we are like Daniel in the den. There's no doubt in my mind that we are in trouble, and like him, we have no way out.

"Strip!"

My heart stops; my muscles seize. My cousin is facing away from me, though she is still in my sight. She's spotted a chance and is off at high speed, shouting:

"Run!"

With that one word, she's through the defences and out to freedom.

I'm frozen to my spot. I can't respond. She's gone, left me; she's not coming back!

Shocked, my eyes fix on the gap she used.

I bolt for it and miraculously find I am through and onto the path.

I've no intention of stopping. My cousin is nowhere to be seen.

I find my new smart slip-on shoes are difficult to run in; my feet are too loose in them. I'm having difficulty keeping them on; they are definitely too big for running. There's nothing I can do about it.

My left shoe is off. I can't take a chance to glance back; the youths might be behind me. I'm too scared to look.

I keep running with awkward, hobbling strides. Over the bridge, along the street and down through the builder's yard, to the garden gate and home.

I'm safe. I've survived.

But I have to face my father, tell him that I've lost my new shoe. I bawl at the very thought of having to say it:

"I've lost my shoe . . ."

The menacing gang, my cousin deserting me, my hobble to safety back home all seem nothing to me compared to the loss of my shoe.

The police are called.

Now the whole family is retracing my steps. Back in the woods, my father spots my shoe high up on a tree branch above the path. I'm so relieved and thankful to see it.

I know if I had gone back, alone, I would never have looked up to find it.

Those lads knew I'd not reach it up there, but at least they didn't hide it; I'm very grateful for that, but I don't share that thought with my parents. The youths frightened me; I don't want to thank them for anything.

My feelings towards my cousin are different, I think, now I know she's prepared to abandon me to the lions.

B35 Unrivalled Interest

Most of the children at Crofton Junior School are off to London today for the Annual School Outing. We are going to the Tower of London.

My class has been divided up into groups, each of about eight children. I happen to be the only girl in my group. I'm very happy with the arrangement as I'm with my teacher, Mr Court. Perhaps it's a mistake, but I'm not going to mention it as I might get moved into a girls' group.

On arriving at The Tower, I don't notice any building that I have in my imagination or that I've seen in pictures.

We file off the coach and go down steps inside a basement. It's dimly lit. Slowly we move forward in a tight queue. Eventually we pass different crowns and other jewelled objects. It takes a long time as there are many other school children going along these narrow underground corridors. I know I should be interested in what we are looking at but I'm not; I want to be outside in the sunshine, looking at the black ravens.

Ever since we were told about the ravens that live in the grounds of the Tower, I've been looking forward to watching them up close. I really wanted to see them first as I've never seen a raven before.

Being down here is cramped and tedious; my mind is not down here, it's outside with the magnificent birds.

There are no windows, so I can't even look out. This isn't how I imagined a trip to the Tower of London would be. Where is the Tower? When will we see it? I can tell the boys in my group feel the same way, but at least they are taller and can see the objects properly. I'm the shortest in my class, which normally never bothers me.

Out at last; now I will be able to see what really interests me.

These huge ravens come very near to us. I can't take my eyes off them. Their beaks are thickly set and very broad; their eyes flash continually. They bob their heads when they strut forwards. Their walking makes me laugh; they do not hop like other birds I know.

They seem very alert, as if they are thinking all the time. I expect the ravens want to stay here because they are fed regularly; it looks as though they are free to leave if they want. They have no ties holding them, and I see no cages.

Feeding them from our packed lunches is not permitted. Where do they sleep?

Before I left home today, I was given my very own camera, a black Brownie 127. It has a rust-brown canvas case with a popper to keep its top flap in place. There is a thin cord on the camera keeping it safe around my neck. It would be easy to lose the nice case, as when it is off the camera, it could get lost.

A little window on the back of the camera shows the number 1. The film was put in the camera at home in the dark, so I don't know how it was done. I mustn't open the back as that would let in the light and ruin the whole film, my father told me.

I'm very proud to have my own camera.

I press the knob to take my very first photograph, trying not to press down too hard and blur the picture. I ask Mr Court to wind it on to the next number. He shows me how to do this to reach number 2 in the window. It's very important, he tells me, that the number is in the middle of the window.

I took the first picture of a raven when he was up close to me, and the second is of the plaque fixed to a large rock which tells visitors about the ravens. I hope to be able to read it later at home.

With the two photos in my Brownie 127, I arrive home.

My father seems puzzled.

"Why take only two when I put a new film in your new camera?

"Only the ravens really interested me. But I do know how to wind it on," I insist. "Mr Court showed me."

Nothing else appeared that interested me as much as the ravens. I didn't see the Tower, so I didn't waste any of my film; each one, i believed to be precious.

I decided it was better to save the others for another time, that's all.

B36 Holiday Confinement

The boot of the car and the roof rack are both packed with what we will need for our camping holiday. We are heading for Appledore in North Devon.

My sisters and I always sleep in a large ridge tent, while my parents share a smaller one. A third tent is used as a cooking and eating space, in case it rains.

We eat with our plates resting on our laps, sitting on folding stools around the primus stoves.

As soon as we arrive, I have the task of fetching hay to fill my palliasse. I find it softer than the straw we've used on previous holidays. Mother sewed our long cotton bags on the sewing machine. Once filled, but not too full, they make a comfortable place to sleep in the tent, all three of us side by side.

There's not much room for anything else, so things get stored under the flaps of the flysheet that hang out from the sides of our tent.

My parents sleep on two army camp beds, wooden with green stretched canvas.

The field we are in is quite close to the farm sheds; the milking parlour isn't that far away. This is not a campsite as such; we are the only campers on the farm.

I guess my father makes our holiday arrangements before we arrive because he never has to search for these places; he drives straight in.

There will be something near here that he wishes to visit, I guess; it's usually a castle that we will all spend time at.

I love watching the milking of the cows in the parlour during the afternoon; I'm never up in time to make it to the morning's milking. After the milk is collected in pails from the cows, it is brought to the cooling parlour; it is still warm and has to be cooled before it is bottled.

Cold water runs inside a thin, upright, metal container. Its back and front are formed with waves in the metal so the fresh warm milk, when it is poured from the top, travels down over the outside of the cooled metal. It stands higher than me. I watch the milk with fascination as it travels evenly down and over the ridges of the cooler; there's never a break in the white pattern. It looks like a block of solid milk. It's hard to tell it is moving, it runs so evenly.

It's a clever idea for cooling the milk. All the metal equipment is made of thick stainless steel and is washed in great troughs within the parlour during milking. The clattering that the metal makes never disturbs the cows.

Once cooled, the milk is bottled and capped with cardboard tops that tell customers where the milk bottles belong. The bottled milk is put into crates for delivery locally.

Some of the milk is kept aside to stand. The cream settles eventually on the top; it is skimmed off to be churned into butter in a special container. Butter pats are used to shape the butter into blocks before it is packed.

My visits to the parlour have been stopped today as all three of us have mumps. We are confined to our tent, maybe for several days.

This is not quite how I imagined I would spend our holiday, lying in a tent with a swollen throat.

B37 What Happened?

The car is unpacked from our holiday.

Father has come in from the back garden. He's not in a happy mood.

"The peach has gone."

I can feel his loss. He was very proud weeks ago when he came in from the back garden announcing that a single peach was forming.

It grew against the warm fence and was surprisingly large considering it was growing outside in our country, he told me. It was at my eye level so I could study it as the weeks went by; I watched it swelling and changing colour until it began to look like one sold in the greengrocer's.

Now my father has arrived home to find it gone. Nothing else is said.

What happened to it, I wonder?

Today, Thomas has squeezed through the gap in the fence at the bottom of the garden.

There are too many fruit bushes back here for anyone to notice us busy digging a hole under one of the gooseberry bushes.

It has to be deep enough to take the square tin I have found to hold the blackbird I came upon this morning; it's dead and very stiff. Thomas is helping me give it a proper burial.

Once Thomas has returned to his home, I shall settle down under the farthest away gooseberry bush where some of the fruit has been missed. I spotted them while we were burying the blackbird.

I find that between the thorny branches right underneath near the ground are huge, juicy gooseberries, golden brown and very soft. I feel that they won't be missed if I eat them. If anyone calls me, I will hear them.

It's not uncomfortable to sit under the fruit bushes because they are not weeded, so it's not like sitting on the soil.

I've not eaten many when I spot what looks like a large flat stone amongst the weeds under another bush. It looks rather out of place, so I get up to take a closer look.

To my utter surprise, I find it is a tortoise! I've never seen one in real life before, only in books.

It's about the size of a tea plate. I don't expect it to be very heavy to pick up.

It really does look like a stone now, as its head and legs are out of sight. It's far heavier than I thought, and its belly is hard, not soft and warm like the belly of a hedgehog.

I carry it down to the kitchen.

"That will be someone's."

I find him a box. I shall go to all the houses nearby until I find his home. He must have lost his way.

B38 Essential Mission

With the tortoise safely in a box, I set off with my younger sister to look for its home. I guess it might not live in Ash

Close as gardens that don't belong to Ash Close houses back onto ours, like the very end of Thomas's.

I've never been to the front of Thomas's house, so I may have passed it without knowing it.

I've already found out he doesn't belong to Thomas; he's never spotted him in his garden, so I'm going to look towards the gardens on the other side from him.

He definitely doesn't belong to our immediate neighbour, but what house does her garden back onto?

It's a grand mystery tour as we now feel miles away from our garden and haven't yet found anyone who owns a tortoise. Some people make suggestions, but these leads haven't got us anywhere so far.

I have no idea how the tortoise's garden is linked with ours:

"Thank you! Yes, he's ours."

I immediately smile broadly at my success in finding the tortoise's home and hand over the box. My perseverance has paid off.

There's no quick way back home as no garden gates link the gardens at the back.

However, the tortoise doesn't take long to return!

This will now be the third time I've returned it. Something must be attracting it, for it to decide that it wants to keep making the long, slow journey. It's a mystery to everyone, so I don't have an answer. My sister has long lost interest, so I walk around alone.

"We think you should keep it."

Golly. I was never expecting that!

I proudly take it home with me.

B39 Attempt Aborted

A fair-sized van has pulled up in Ash Close.

If the onion man arrives on his bicycle when my father is around, the two men have quite a chat.

He is distinctively dressed in a navy-blue beret, with a red neck-a-chief; strings of huge onions hang from his handlebars. I've never heard his voice as my father chats out on the road when he goes to collect his onions from the bicycle. The onion man is dressed to look French, but he may be a man who lives in Petts Wood. The strings of onions would be hung in the garage. They always look identical; they never look real.

I'm used to the horses of the coal man, rag-and-bone man and milkman coming into Ash Close but not a van. Where is it heading?

The van is now backing up towards our garage doors. We have no gates.

I'm soon understanding the significance of the van. It's for furniture!

Mother is directing the proceedings as one item after the other is loaded. I guess that when all the chosen pieces are safely aboard, we too will all be loaded.

There's not too much time for further thought because at the end of the Close, a black car has turned down. It's my father.

I'm keeping well out of it, but curiosity has me peeking to see where he will park now that the space in front of the garage is occupied. Whoops! He's parked at a strange angle across the front of the van, half on the drive and half on the pavement. I think he's trying to say something!

Item by item, things are unloaded and placed back where they came from. The furniture is staying in the house after all. I wonder where my mother was heading?

I hear no more about it except that it was the neighbour next door that alerted my father while he was at work.

My hand is up to my mouth, hiding a cringe, as I imagine my father in full flow: his class of boys engrossed in the History master's lesson, then a knock and the school secretary enters, passing a brief note and leaves. What then?

How can a master leave a class of pupils in mid-flow to rush back home to stop his house being emptied . . . by his wife! Perhaps the note said "burglars" rather than "wife". Perhaps the neighbour imagined it was a robbery going on next door.

Anyway, it didn't work, whatever plan had been hatched. A smaller van may have worked? My mother no longer has a good word for the neighbour.

B40 Birthday Pyjamas

My mother knits, sews on the machine, plays the piano on occasion and goes to pottery classes.

Jumpers, socks and mittens knitted with four needles. Her many bags of wool are kept in the cupboard under the stairs, along with our wellington boots. A tall wicker laundry basket is stuffed with spare wool; there are twisted skeins and many hand-wound balls. I am often given the task of untwisting a skein and stretching it out round my wrists. My mother then winds it into a ball. It's easier to knit a garment once the wool is in a ball.

My mother is sewing on the machine, out in the garage; she's sewing in secret while my father is out. The garage is a good place for secretly using the machine. Things can be packed and stowed away quickly. I imagine the garage has been used before in this way.

The garment now in progress in the garage is a pair of men's pyjamas, fleecy brushed cotton with muted stripes of blue, pink, and white.

The pyjamas are to be a surprise birthday present for my father, his birthday being soon, on Christmas Day.

Almost complete and with just the buttons on the pyjama-top needed, my mother announces that she's put the buttonholes on the wrong side, as if made for a woman to button up, and that was bound to annoy my father when he realises.

If she has made a mistake, I feel she has brushed it aside far too quickly. I think my mother is good at engineering trouble when she wants to. Is this what she has done? It feels like that to me but I would never talk abut it.

B41 Personal Pride

Mr Court, my class teacher, will soon be finishing the morning lesson. Then we will have our lunch here as our classroom is also the school canteen. I love my school dinners.

Mr Court comes over to where I am sitting and quietly tells me that I'm needed after I've eaten my dinner; I have to go to the hut that houses the stage. It's in this hut that plays and concerts are performed for the parents.

I've never been asked to go there before, so I'm rather curious to know what it is about; I didn't ask, so I'm eating my shepherd's pie and gypsy tart wondering what Mr Court's message was all about.

I reach the steps to the hut. I don't see anyone else around so I go up alone. Inside I find a small group of boys and girls; there's no one I know here. We wait, quietly chatting about what this might be about, without anyone coming to tell us why we have been gathered.

We are now asked to file up the steps at the side of the stage and onto its wooden stage floor.

I see a trestle table set up at the back of the stage; it looks as though it has come from my classroom; it's similar to the large folding tables that are set up for the dinners. These tables are long and strong but they can be folded and transported easily. This one has no long benches for sitting; it stands alone.

On this table is a row of bells rather like the one used by a teacher in the playground; it is rung outside to tell us to line up for class at the end of playtime. The school bell has a large wooden handle, whereas these have wide leather straps to hold. There are different sizes, so it looks like there are bells for all ages.

The teacher explains the sounds of the different bells. She then asks us to take a bell. Carefully holding it still, we line up facing her.

I can't wait to try mine. I love the sound of the school bell; that is the only bell I know, except that of a fire engine and church bells occasionally.

One by one, in turn, we ring our bell just once. Each sound echoes around the walls of the hut. I can't believe I've been included in this group, but I'm very happy to be here.

My bell's sound, I learn, fits into a tune she wants us to try, so we are lined up in such a way to play three blind mice. We all know the tune, so it's not too difficult. I soon get to know the special sound of my bell, so I know when I must ring it.

Some bells have to be rung twice, but it's not difficult to know that your bell has to be rung again; as long as you know the tune, it's easy. Everyone's part is special, so each ring is important; to daydream and miss one's part would be a disaster.

The school is to perform a Christmas Pantomime this term: *Dick Whittington*.

We are given the task of ringing a peal of bells during the performance. We are to start our peal as Dick Whittington arrives in London.

We are in the wings off-stage, out of sight, but our bells sound loud and clear to the whole audience.

I wouldn't want to be ringing my bell in front of the audience; being behind the curtains is enjoyable. We all take this task seriously. Each of us is needed to make the peal run smoothly. Everyone has an important role to play in the pantomime. I feel proud to be included.

Who would have thought that I would be taking part in the Christmas Pantomime? I still find it hard to believe. There are only a handful of us out of the whole school; I've no idea why I should have been chosen to be a lucky one.

B42 Unplanned Event

Christmas is coming! The utility dining table has extra leaves added so that all of us can fit around it comfortably come Christmas day. At this moment, it is strewn with coloured papers.

We three children are making Christmas paper chains — yards of them. We each have blocks of cut paper strips; they come in all colours of the rainbow. Choose your colour. Lick and stick. Choose again, thread it through, lick and stick. We are busy working peacefully at our task with no end in sight, the pile of paper chains getting higher and higher.

The back garden fence catches the light through the Crittall-framed French doors. There are no curtains across the glass.

To the front of the house is a young cherry tree. I can't see it from this back room.

I love to watch it when the leaves are falling; I lean on the window sill of the bay window on still, cold days, watching the beautiful red-golden leaves fall gently, each waiting for their moment. I'm transfixed. It's as if the tree is crying leaves until there are no more tears left to cry.

Both our parents are out. My father is not yet home from his school. My mother is at the hairdresser's in town, a weekly jaunt for her. Perhaps she's there for a set. If she is having a perm, she will be gone for hours.

It's dark, but not that late. Light from the room is now flooding the few steps outside, then up across the lawn towards where the small gate enters the builder's yard.

The coal fire is lit in the grate. More coal stands in the tall scuttle to the side of the hearth. We are busy here alone making yards of Christmas paper chains. Happy and bothering nobody.

"What's that smell?"

We have coal fires in both rooms downstairs and a tiny green stove in the kitchen near the back door. This is fed coke, never coal.

When the coal man arrives at 6 Ash Close, his horse patiently waits while he delivers. He first drags a sack forward to the edge of his cart before lifting it onto his back, which is covered with a strange heavy apron, blackened with coal dust. It's to stop his shoulders getting black, I think.

His face is also black with coal dust. He goes back and forth, out of sight down our passage by the garage; full sack in, empty sack back. The coke is in larger sacks than the coal.

His Shire horse, always blinkered, with strong shaggy hooves, has his head bowed slightly. Behind his chunky blinkers, his eyes might be closed. He might even snooze while he's waiting, I think. His reins hang loose, but he stays quite still until the coal man is up again, saying the usual:

"Gee-up!"

We are well used to the many smells from the different fires in the house. This smell is a new, different smell. It's not one we can identify; our noses are soon used to it, so it's soon forgotten.

"Look!"

Smoke is seeping under the door from the hallway. It's dark and evenly spread thickly along the bottom of the closed door.

We jump up; the decorations are now abandoned.

I rush to the hall door to have a quick peek, expecting the smoke to be coming from the kitchen; perhaps it's from the little stove,which will be lit as it's been cold today.

I open the door a tiny chink and shut it fast.

"The cupboard's on fire!"

No way can we get out through the kitchen or the front door.

"Try the French doors!"

Two of us are through and up the lawn towards the yard, calling back:

"Come on, *come on!*"

My younger sister stands on the threshold by the flung open French doors.

Screaming and bawling, she's staying put.

Up through the yard, my other sister soon falls over a low trolley, a hand-pulled flatbed kept in the builder's yard. It's dark in the narrow passage. I leave her moaning, hugging her foot; I run on and out of the yard onto the street. I turn right, towards the main area of the town, not knowing which shop is the hairdresser's; I need desperately to find it.

My sister isn't behind me. I've never been to my mother's hairdresser. Where is it?

I'm now close to the Daylight Inn.

Opposite it, I spot a shop window lit, its soft curtaining closed. I'll try the door.

It's open!

I barge in. By chance, it is a hairdresser's! Ladies are having their hair done, all in various stages of completion.

The scene is gently relaxed and peaceful, *Women's Weekly* or *Horse and Hound* spread on their laps while the huge dryers covering their heads are whirring into their ears. Pausing and looking past them all, I spot the back of my mother's head; she's facing away from me into a huge mirror.

I scream at the reflection in the mirror:

"The house is on fire!"

We are packed off to the neighbour's. The youngest is calmed with hot cocoa; bowls of hot water are fetched for the swollen foot. All is well. All are safe. We girls are to stay the night at the neighbour's.

The firemen have saved the house and rescued Tommy the cat.

In the morning, I have a brief view of the burnt-out stairs and the debris from the cupboard piled high on the back lawn. It is still smouldering, and that strange, pungent smell wafts up my nostrils again: the puzzling smell is the wool singeing.

I stare at the huge pile, which is still sending up small spirals of smoke. It's completely unrecognisable, mainly because I see no colour. The pile is black in every nook and cranny. What's also amazing is that this whole pile of black stuff once fitted into the cupboard under the stairs. The firemen must have pulled it all out and piled it here last night.

I can see that the wool tried to burn. The large, tall wicker laundry basket in which it was held is gone, now in ashes somewhere. That old, brittle structure burned well, as did the stairs, but the wool did not. I observe this phenomenon with great thought. I'm gripped with curiosity.

If I were to prod the black, hand-wound balls of wool, would I see some colour inside? I will never know as I'm not going to prod the pile; I'm thinking that it might just answer my question, that's all.

I'm called, distracted from my thoughts. We are going to my grandparents at Windyridge in Wingham and won't be returning for some time. My father has to return here to sort out the mess.

When I hear talk of the fire, I pretend not to listen or be interested.

"The meter is just inside the door . . . could have . . . embers in the boots . ."

True, my mother does put embers from the fire in our wellingtons, but only if we're going to put them on.

Small, hot coals are tonged out of the fire and put straight into the boot, shaken about then rolled out of the boot back into the fire. I am allowed to do some of the shaking. The hot coals have to be kept moving, otherwise they would burn the cream linings of the boot.

I never see my father use this practice. It's one my mother uses. She does it to warm the chilly insides of the wellingtons before we put them on to go outside. Down at Windyridge, they use a warming pan to heat the cold bedding. Hot coals are put in the pan and it is swished in and out of each bed before we get in.

My mother leaving hot embers in the boots is a silly idea. After being outside wearing the wellingtons, we put the boots straight back in the cupboard under the stairs. No stray ember could get in the cupboard that way, I've decided.

If it was an ember in a boot, how did it get into the cupboard?

Lots of ideas fill my head as to how a possible ember got into the cupboard under the stairs. When was it put there? By whom? The French doors were unlocked. We could escape. Were they unlocked ready for that?

It's a mystery story that I share with no one.

Today we are leaving the burnt-out stairs of Ash Close to spend time at Windyridge. My mother is to drive us down the sixty miles; then my father will return with the car to Ash Close. He isn't to pick us up for many weeks.

My greatest joy is always spending Christmas at Windyridge.

Turning off the lane, up into the short drive between the tree-thickened hedges that butt straight onto the road, I'm aroused by the noise of the car tyres on the gravel. My excitement is unbearable. Windyridge is my most favourite place on Earth.

Quick greetings and I will be off to survey the garden, the orchard, the geese and the chickens. Coggy, my aunty Dulcie's cocker spaniel, will be bounding behind me, I'm sure.

I know this visit won't include summer breakfasts out on the lawn by the old cherry tree. Instead, it will be log fires, over which crumpets will be toasted, oozing melted butter dripping down my chin. A brass toasting fork hangs all year by the fireplace, waiting for Christmas.

The oil lamp on the round table will be moved and replaced by the wind-up gramophone. Heavy, brittle 45s will blare out Scottish reels. As the record slows, growing deeper and deeper, someone will rush to wind it up so the dancing can continue.

On lifting the lid of the gramophone, there inside will be the little label of a white dog looking into the big horn: His Master's Voice. He is on most of the records, seen through the perfectly formed holes in the stiff brown paper sleeves. The records will be carefully stored back in their very own upright box.

Cards will be played, and my grandad will challenge me to a game of chess. Big wooden pieces, carved proudly. The castles look real, but the pawns are a strange shape. My grandad taught me how to play one summer.

At Ash Close, there is only one chess set; it is my mother's. Her set is in a neat, polished wooden box, which opens up to reveal all the pieces still in their positions, just as they were when left from the last unfinished game. Each piece has a peg to slot in its square and hold it in place. Half are white, half are red. Unfolding the box wrongly is a disaster as they all fall out of their holes and the game is lost. When folded correctly, the unfinished game is safely put back in the cupboard, to be continued next time.

I will be allowed freely into everything here, no restraints. I will busy myself collecting eggs from the hens after searching hard in the bushes, and stacking newly split wood near the house. If it were summer, I'd be cleaning the stone bird bath and shaking my bedding out in the garden each morning, after flinging open the French doors where I sleep.

We have arrived; the car has stopped. I'm bursting to get out!

B43 Christmas Heaven

Hugs now over, I run quickly through every room in Windyridge, checking on any changes. I want it all as before. I feel comfortable with my memories of everything; with those in my head, I feel as if I have never left.

I'm happy with things around me with their chips and scratches. I'd sooner they were like that than to find they have been thrown away, replaced with something different. I can get used to additions as long they aren't replacing the old and familiar.

My home at Ash Close has few of these feelings; I don't miss it or feel I need it.

The Windyridge front door has no hallway; it opens straight into the front room. A wire cage hangs behind the high-up letter box to catch the post. Coggy, who likes chewing up letters, can't snatch them from the cage. This cage is big enough to catch rats, but now it just catches the post.

Straight ahead is the fireplace, arched and bricked decoratively; little cubby holes are formed in the brickwork either side of the surround. Each cubby hole has a wooden lining. They are practical places, housing such things as matches and candles.

On little hooks in the brickwork are hung horse brasses from the days when Shire horses were kept on the farm. The family were founder members of the Shire Horse Society. One brass I particularly like is of a prancing horse. It's the Horse of Kent, my grandad tells me.

Cherry wood is stacked in the orchard. In the big wooden barn, it is split, chopped and brought, eventually, into the room when needed; there might also be apple wood. Both, when burning, will fill the room with a sweet smell.

Grandad's chunk of a chopping block is seriously criss-crossed with axe marks. Stored in the apex of the barn roof is, hanging, an old canoe. The shell is constructed of curved timbers. Areas of its old stretched canvas hang sadly above our heads. It's in a very dusty, neglected state. It belongs on the water, not in its overhead grave, sadly wilting.

Standing beneath the canoe, I can watch the pig swill being stirred by Grandad in the old pail. I enjoy the warm, mealy smell it gives off. Or else I watch grandad turning a new leg on the wood-lathe for the three-legged table in the front room.

In the living room are lots of comfortable chairs with loose cushions, and a large, dark, almost black, oak sideboard, Jacobean style with cupboards and shelves top and bottom. It is deeply carved and very hefty.

Above in the centre of it is a small door with a heavily carved panel, butted by turned wooden pillars reaching down to the surface, on which things are stood. On either side stand two large Worcester vases decorated with gentle pictures of cattle, trees and streams. Both scenes are of cows but are slightly different, hand-painted pictures. They were made in the Worcester factory near where my granny's family lived in Lower Wick. Their farm grew hops.

There are numerous smaller Wedgewood items on the sideboard. One is a biscuit barrel with a blue and white raised decoration. With its silver drop handle, it stands near the telephone. It no longer holds biscuits, just odds and ends.

Often, in the summer, a huge vase filled with lupins, delphiniums and sprays of sweet-smelling mock orange is placed in the centre of the sideboard. Any array of flowers can be collected in the summer. Some are never picked: Californian poppies, marigolds, periwinkle and evening primrose; thes are left growing wherever they fancy. I'm told some flowers don't last long when picked.

There's an absence of utility furniture at Windyridge. Most items have come down through the family. It is a feast for my eyes, a museum of interesting, absorbing things: old books, oil paintings and very large framed photographs: Grandad, dressed for the hunt upon his fine horse, hounds waiting for the signal to be off, which will sound from the bugle he is holding. In the photograph, he was: "Master of the Hunt" at the time.

Grandad's bugle needs enormous puff; it's impossible for me to raise even the smallest squeak. It hangs beneath the huge photograph showing the hunt about to set off in Wingham.

In the front room, the large oil lamp sits centre stage on the three-legged round table. My grandad will light the lamp after sunset tonight. After carefully trimming the wicks, he will light many smaller lamps for all the dark spots in Windyridge. Nightlights can be picked up and carried around safely to wherever they are needed.

On arriving, I want to head straight to the cupboard in the back hallway; this is before my checking begins. There are two doors side by side in the passage wall; the one on the right is the walk-in larder with its tiny window of netted metal to stop things from flying in.

Uncooked meat is kept outside in a free-standing cupboard; it has very strong metal mesh sides to allow cold air to waft through and keep rodents out. It's referred to as the "meat safe". It is positioned near the outside tap, which has become green-coated with age. The back door is off the small scullery where food is prepared and washing up done. This is very much my grandad's space. It's rare for any of the women to go down to the scullery. It has few cupboards, lots of shelves holding all manner of things. Above the low stone sink is the only window in the room. The little window overlooks the asparagus bed lying beyond the path which runs around to the front porch.

The door to the left of the larder is where I'm heading; it holds numerous things: playing cards, Snakes and Ladders, the croquet set, a spare camp bed, a dart board and heavy wooden tennis rackets trapped in hefty clamps to keep them from getting out of shape.

Shelved and full to the brim. I'm straight to the cupboard to fetch my favourite teddy, not the one in the best shape, blind in his left eye, but he's the one I want.

My pleas of "Can I take him home?" get no reply. I no longer ask. He will stay with me now until I'm ready to climb into the car to go home, when I will hand him back.

The two huge rooms further on past the "play" cupboard is where all our beds have been set up. Folding wooden camp beds, each with stretched canvas, lots of woollen blankets and eiderdowns. There are no fires at this end; it's very cold away from the wood fire and the Rayburn.

The trusty, soft green Rayburn is in a small room with a large oak table; we all squeeze around it to have our meals.

Tonight, before we climb into bed, the warming pan will be taken off the wall and filled with wood embers from the front-room fire. With its long handle, it will be moved up and down under my blankets. A hot water bottle, too, will be in my bed. I will snuggle down with Teddy after my cocoa.

These two back rooms make one very big one when the central doors are folded back. Plenty of light flows in through the window stretching the length of the long thinly built wall, looking towards the gravel drive. There is no space for a window sill, so nothing can stand there. This vast space, built from wood, is called "the new rooms" as it was added sometime after the main building.

Windyridge was built for Granny and Grandad. Designed and built on land within Grandad's family farm, it stands next to the oast house where the hops were dried. The bungalow is surrounded by plenty of gardens. Adjoining is a three-acre orchard of mainly cherry trees, beyond which is a walled kitchen garden growing very young fruit trees.

My grandad's father was a farmer, as was my grandad. Grandad no longer farms. All the farmland is tenanted, as are all the farm buildings. I've never been inside them. I'd like to see inside the oast house, which stands next door, as I can't imagine how it would look inside.

The family are well known in Wingham village. Family history is in all the photographs on the walls; there are sketches and paintings, embroideries too, mostly done by my granny's family members. All the objects hold part of a story that reveals itself in tiny snippets.

My aunty Jean and aunty Dulcie share a bedroom in the older part of the bungalow. All Dulcie's dressmaking things are set up in the "new rooms": the machine, the dummy and the cutting table.

Aunty Dulcie carries out her work at home, in Windyridge; she's a "dressmaker". This actually includes all types of clothing.

My aunty Jean used to lecture at university but now her illness keeps her at home. I see her in her ill state rarely but I know that it's unpredictability would mean she couldn't take a job. Her behaviour can change drastically; I don't see a reason for these changes.

The household is always busy doing something or other. I get involved in the summer; we sit under the porch by the front door with the sun streaming in, topping and tailing gooseberries or stringing runner beans. The porch houses two bench seats. We share a big saucepan which sits on the ground between us. There are always plenty of such things to do. Life is never dull.

I feel alive here. The stifling atmosphere of 6 Ash Close is long forgotten. Four acres to safely play; few cars passing along the lane, hidden by the tall hedge. Nothing beyond the hedge to entice me away; out beyond the wide wooden farm gate of the drive, belongs to another world.

I can disappear for hours within the Windyridge grounds, until the shout goes up for tea.

While staying this long at Windyridge following the fire at Ash Close, I have to go to a school close by. It is a small, old building with just a few teachers, a tiny school compared with Crofton. The main room where we are taught has a stoked stove in the middle, with a strong mesh fence forming a guard. Wet clothes can be hung to dry.

This morning we are all given 11 Plus test examples to see if we can work them out.

I'm not sure how long I will be at this school, but it's long enough for me to realise that the 11 Plus is fast approaching for real; perhaps we will all be "sitting" it fairly soon, much like my older sister did two years ago.

My father has arrived unexpectedly to take us all back to Ash Close; Teddy is given up. My long stay here has ended without a single word of warning.

Windyridge has no car, television or electricity; just the telephone: Wingham 109.

When it rings, it is quite an event. I can recognise the shout even when I'm right up in the orchard:

"Telephone!"

Everyone in the household knows when a call comes through. Had there been one from my father to plan our departure? If there was one, when had it been? I knew nothing about it.

We're now back home. There's no evidence of the fire; not in the house, nor the garden. A miracle has been performed. The smell in the hallway is now of new wood, plaster and paint. The burnt wool stench has gone completely. Seeing this transformation, I start to feel as though the fire was a dream.

Did my father really change the charred, pungent scene? I'm starting to doubt this, though; my father is not a handyman. He plays cricket, reads *The Times* and studies history.

I'm dropped off at Crofton School by my father which is most unusual; no walk to school today. It's my first morning back after my long spell at Windyridge. I head for my classroom.

Arrangements, I find, are now different. Everyone else must know what is happening today, except me:

We are all to sit the 11 Plus!

Was this the reason for the sudden rush to get us home?

My head is in a whirl. There'll be odd questions to fathom out, no doubt. I'm not bothered. I decide if I fail, it will mean I will go to a different school from my sister. Failing won't be so bad, knowing that would be the outcome.

The promised new bicycle from my father is the last thing on my mind.

The test is done and I'm relieved it's over. With any luck, all the bombardment from my father, of mental arithmetic, spelling and times-table testing will stop now. Picnics will be carefree again.

The results have arrived.

My spirits are high today; my father's, I guess, are not so jovial. I struggled; tried my best. Failing when you have tried is okay, I feel.

B44 World Encroached

I know my half-mile walk to Crofton School very well. Not far from home, I call for Pauline. We then walk the rest of the way together. I knock at her front door and her father comes to show me in. The timing of the door opening is always the same. It never changes. I am directed into a room on the right where I stand and wait. I never sit to wait as it might disturb the chair covers.

The clock on the mantelpiece has a polished case forming a perfect arch over the clock face. It proudly looks out, ticking slowly and loudly. It looks like an eye with a perfect eyebrow.

Hands, face, and a brow; such a mix of things just for a clock. It dongs once while I wait, but I know it isn't one o'clock. It only ever chimes once.

Beneath the mantelpiece is an all-night burner. Fine slack is piled in the grate; it is high and neatly arranged. A few small whiffs of smoke escape up the chimney. The fire seems to say to me, "I am sleeping; wake me later."

Nothing feels hurried here. The peace is never disturbed. Every morning is the same. No noise; everything is still in place as if it is never touched. The clock dongs, the fire smokes; no other life is stirring. I know in a moment the door will open and I will turn and walk through it to the front door where Pauline will be waiting, facing me, from outside.

Tomorrow I will knock again; the door will open, the fire will gently smoke and the clock will chime once. It's a clockwork house, I've decided.

Outside, the street is straight with perfectly identical houses on either side. Hedges trimmed, door knockers polished and windows cleaned.

Far down the end of the street I see the moon, huge and nestling down among the rooftops. It glows orange and full. Why is it there? Why so low? How out of place it looks now, resting among the houses. As we cross the road, it slips away and out of sight.

Being there at that moment was just the right time for me, not too early, not too late.

We cross over a railway bridge. I'm hoping a train will pass under and I will be engulfed by the distinct smell from the steam. The boys in my class say the bridge would collapse if one of its bricks at the top of the arch were removed. I hope they don't plan to do it.

On nearing school, I get a shock.

My mother, in a black peaked cap and white coated official uniform, is holding a "lollipop" in the centre of the road. Is it really her? I feel embarrassed.

Pauline doesn't know it's my mother. I cross the road assisted by my mother, but I barely acknowledge her.

I want to know about such changes before they happen. I didn't like this surprise; I don't want to be thinking about it.

I will think about the wonderful moon instead.

B45 Life's Frustrations

My mother has not had a job since I can remember. I don't mind that, but I wish she'd gone to another school to work, that's all. She's too near my world. School is school, home is home for me, and I'm happy if my parents keep well away. My mother now appearing near my school gate and being there daily does not please me at all. I tell no one that I know the lollipop lady.

I don't know the process of achieving such work but my mother does not hide her considerable achievement; from her viewpoint her job is with the Metropolitan Police and she is very proud of her position.

Throughout my earlier Crofton school years, I was having to follow my sister. She's over two years older than me so she changed schools some time ago. I'm no longer someone's sister thank goodness.

Going on an errand to another class is something I love to do; I'm proud to be chosen and entrusted with the message. My moment used to be spoilt though, by the teacher I was delivering the message to, smiling at me and saying:

"I know whose sister you are!"

I don't want to be anyone's sister; I want to be me. Walking in her shadow leaves me no space in my head; she is always able to push into my world uninvited. I longed to be unconnected with anyone while I was in school.

One day on coming home, I heard her talking with my mother about her craft work and history lesson. I listened. I wanted to be in that top class, making models, or sewing table mats. I was compelled to butt in and fib about what I'd been doing at school; my imagination on such occasions was inclined to run away.

My sister spoke of making a model of an Elizabethan house with an overhanging top floor. She'd been painting on beams and criss-crossing a pattern on the windows; the roof was painted in squares for tiles.

I was prompted to say that I had cut out and arranged my tiles like the scales of a fish; that my beams were made of cardboard, cut out, painted and stuck on. All the time my talking continued, I was building a house in my mind, but I described it to them as if I'd been doing it in my class.

My compulsion to fib, compelled by my sister talking about her interesting school activities, knew no bounds because I wanted to do the things she was doing: make the house she is making, sew the cross stitch runner which she brought home to work on.

I was told that I was too young, but my thinking and my ideas told me I was not too young. I could do those things then, if only I was given the chance. I never fibbed about things I was too young to do.

Nobody was interested in my thoughts. There was never a pause to listen to me. It was as if I was not here.

B46 Secretive Furniture

My mother is planning to walk today across Petts Wood from Ash Close to visit a previous neighbour in Farringdon Avenue. She lives further down from Mr Harper.

This lady's front sitting room is darkened by the overgrowth of bushes, so the sunshine never reaches into the front room where we are taken to sit. When we lived on her road, our room was light. We didn't have high bushes near our front windows as she has.

Tea is brought in on a tray with special fairy cakes; perhaps she knew we were coming.

After the two adults have drunk tea, handed around the cakes and chatted adult talk, the lady goes over to a piece of furniture which stands alone against the back wall of the room. She removes a framed photograph that stands all by itself on the top and lifts the large lid of the chest. I think it will be packed with winter clothes or woollen blankets and that the smell of mothballs will soon reach my nostrils.

Down the front of the large lidded box, I can make out sections of cloth held in place with strips of darker wood. The wooden surfaces are highly polished. It looks new and very modern. As it stands alone against the wall, it feels as though this piece of furniture is quite special. She raises the lid with reverence. No unpleasant mothball smells reach me.

I can't see what's inside as I'm still sitting on the settee under the window. My mother has risen and is listening intently, looking and discussing what is inside the chest. I've never seen my mother so focused on a piece of furniture and its contents.

An upended, blue-sleeved record is lifted from inside the chest. At Windyridge, records are stored on their ends too but in a much smaller case which has a handle so that it can be easily carried to be put in and out of a cupboard. It's a heavy case when it is full of a dozen or so records, mostly 78s and a few 45s.

This record is gently slipped from its sleeve.

I'm up to see what is now happening to the record.

Inside the furniture, it is balanced on a spike slid through its centre hole and kept there by a metal swinging arm. The lid is closed and we all sit again. No words now; the room is silent.

There's a plop in the chest. They both laugh. It's the record falling into place all by itself. Suddenly a loud musical chord resounds, bouncing off the four walls of the sparsely furnished room.

An orchestra fills the room with music.

Everyone grins with amazement, me too! What a moment when that sound begins: Brahms; it's one of his well-known *Hungarian Rhapsodies*.

Record after record is played. No winding up to do, and no needle needing to be replaced. Several records can be piled together on the spike. They plop down and play one after the other. The music continues to play with no one needing to move from their seats.

My mother is invited to visit again to listen to more records. We hear *Peer Gynt*, then *The Carnival of the Animals* and *Peter and the Wolf*.

B47 Unwelcome Guest

Mother's cousin Charlotte lives on the road along which I walk to school.

Aunty Charlotte and her husband, "Fluff", live in a rambling house with large rooms. It is surrounded by ground that has numerous large trees. They prevent light flooding into the rooms downstairs. It's not so much a house within a garden as a house standing among trees.

The downstairs is full of interesting things. I've never been upstairs, but I imagine it is the same. There's little space left on the walls when I look up from the bottom of the wide staircase.

They have a Tourer, a car with a soft-topped roof; it is kept in the old garage. We seldom visit, so I can't say that I know aunty Charlotte well. Fluff is hardly ever around.

I know nothing of all the objects or from where they came, but the flavour is of Windyridge: a mixture of all sorts, possibly handed down through the family. Either that or these things were collected on their various exotic travels.

It might be a dark house but inside it is very interesting; it's so different from Ash Close.

Aunty Charlotte wears flamboyant clothes as if she has just emerged from sitting for a painter in his studio. Perhaps they are artists.

The colours inside her house and its decor are gentle and muted, much like the paintings on the walls; nothing garish or startling. It's a timeless place to visit that flows without change.

Charlotte and Fluff adore their two beautiful, long-haired Persian cats. There's no evidence of any children.

On our walk back from visiting aunty Charlotte, a dog comes bounding up to us.

Perhaps this friendly dog can smell the cats. He wants to play.

Without a collar, it's not possible to know whether he has an owner. My mother decides he must come home with us. We are all happy with the idea; he trots with us without any encouragement.

My mother tells us that her family is never without a dog. Even now, there is a dog at Windyridge: Coggy, the cocker spaniel.

Ash Close feels different now with the dog at home with us. There is a focus on its needs. Where is it to sleep? What food should we buy for it? How many walks should it have? I'm hoping, as we all are, that it has no owner. We hope it is a stray. If it is, then it has a home with us.

My father comes through the front door. It's early evening.

"The dog has to go. *Out!*"

My father spent no time getting to know the dog as we did. It stood no chance, sadly. It's highly likely his Bickley home never housed a dog.

B48 Special Delivery

A piece of furniture has now arrived at 6 Ash Close complete with its polished surround and material grill, not unlike the one I saw at the lady's house in Farringdon Avenue where my mother and I recently visited. The tiny little plaque on the front of ours reads "Ferguson".

It is a radiogram. It has been given pride of place in the front room where visitors gather.

It is always my mother who attends to the radiogram; my father shows no interest. It is she who buys the records and plays them.

Rachmaninoff's *Variations on a Theme of Paganini* is now played over and over. Two sides of a small 45 record, so she has to turn it over when the first side has finished. The machine doesn't do that.

More records have followed that first purchase. Not a great flourish, more a slow trickle; always my mother's choice. I don't know what music my father is fond of.

My older sister has had the occasional record purchase made for her: Kathleen Ferrier singing "What is Life to Me without Thee?" On the other side is "Art Thou Troubled?"

I head for the door when my sister's hand reaches into the record case. It's a complete mystery to me as to why anyone would want to listen to these two songs. This lady's voice is deep and the tunes are slow and dreary. Walking away to do other things is my answer; nobody questions that.

My mother's choice is always orchestral, with memorable tunes that I don't mind hearing in my head when the record has been put back in the case.

B49 Further Frustrations

My older sister is to be taken to Covent Garden to see the ballet *Swan Lake*. I want to go, and I say so.

"You are too young."

I never take kindly to these words. I think they get spoken to shut me up and to avoid any further talk on the subject. What age do I have to be, then? When will I not be too young? Next to my sister, I will always be too young, I think.

Mother has lots of Tchaikovsky's ballet music: *The NutcrackerSuite* and *Swan Lake*. I know all the tunes; it's just not fair to not include me.

B50 Tall Request

Crofton School is wonderful. I'm knitting a navy blue scarf with a chessboard effect but no change of colours in the squares, just a change in the look of the stitches.

French knitting, too, using a wooden cotton reel with four small nails hammered in the top. I hook the wool over the tiny nails in a certain order. I can use all manner of spare wool in different colours; there's no shortage of pieces at home.

From the long tail that magically gets longer and longer out of the bottom of the reel when I tug it, I can coil and sew small mats and egg cosies.

Some of the longer pieces of wool are used in the playground to play Cat's Cradle. I had to learn the skill from older children. Then I had to find someone to play with me, someone who knew how to do it. Cat's Cradle only needs one length of wool tied at its ends, which then gets passed back and forth in different patterns which are formed by hooking the fingers in different ways.

Playtime is always a wonderful time when so much is going on. Certain marbles are of great value to their owners; mine are small and ordinary but I still like the swirly coloured glass inside them. I didn't win these as some do; nor do I have any of the really large marbles; they are known as whoppers.

Fivestones is a game that has to be purchased. Then there's Jacks. Lots of little spiked metal pieces and a small rubber ball, all kept safely in a little draw-string bag. There is a skill to doing well with them. Jacks are very popular. I saved my pocket money and bought some from a shop in town.

Skipping in groups requires great timing. Some bring in long ropes they can swing wide, so pairs or a greater number can skip in the turning rope together. Timing is everything. Sometimes a queue is ready and waiting for a turn to head into the turning rope. No marks if it is you who stops the rope with an ill-timed foot; a collective groan, a laugh, and you're out!

Pogo sticks and stilts are the next crazes to hit the playground.

I've never had a pogo stick bought for me, though I would dearly like one.

Some children are lucky; their fathers make really tall stilts for them. They appear above the bushes like clowns at the circus. What must it feel like to be so tall? Seeing everything around from up high must be so different. I'd love to know what it feels like.

I'm lucky — my father is making me some stilts now. I described exactly how I wanted them made as I've been able to look hard to see how the homemade ones are done.

I have a pair of quite tall ones, but they never go to school. I love those the most. The first shorter pair I can take to school as I can carry them under my arm.

Hula-hooping is beyond me. I don't ever request one of those; it's more difficult than it looks.

Stamp swapping and cigarette card collecting is mainly popular with the boys, as skipping and cat's cradle are with the girls. I have my stamp album, but it stays at home.

In the town, I can buy used stamps in little cellophane packets; they come from all over the world. Sorting them into the right countries so they are stuck on the right pages takes time. It's often not straightforward.

B51 Inspired Action

I'm drawn away from some of the joys of the playground by a new club which I hear is starting up. It is to be in one of the larger huts, one I've never been in before.

The whole school is made of huts. Dark creosoted wood. There have to be a few steps up to each hut door because the huts are all raised off the ground. If ever a ball rolls under, you have to crawl beneath to fetch it. Luckily, there are small stones spread under the huts so the ball doesn't roll too far under.

Up the steps, in the centre of most huts, is a small lobby; then a door on both sides, each to a classroom.

Mine is just one big hut though, as at 12 o'clock it becomes the school canteen where we all eat our school dinners.

The club is in a hut far across the other side of the school from mine. I have to pass a hut where I once wet myself in class. I'd just moved up from the infants' school, which was not laid out in class rows as it is here. I was too inhibited to put my hand up to ask if I could leave the room for the toilet l wasn't afraid of the teacher; I just didn't want to draw attention to myself. I had no idea where that was to lead.

The warm trickle down my leg was the first I knew that it was actually happening; it had surprised me that I hadn't had a signal at the start of the trickle. Wetting myself was not something I would ever have done if I could have controlled it happening.

I ignored the growing pool, but as I was slowly being surrounded by a big puddle, the teacher couldn't help but notice. After that happened to me, I could understand how it happens to others. Adults are never angry about the interruption it causes, so they must understand too.

Everyone is sitting on top of the desks when I enter the club hut so it doesn't look like a class lesson is set up. All ages are mixed up. I look around; I know no one. I sit on a desk by myself near the front, expectant and very quietly waiting, as we all are.

I don't know the teacher. He starts talking about the sea, how calm and flat it is on this still day. We are told to imagine. All eyes are closed.

He describes the peace of the water as it gently laps at the boat. The weather is changing; some dark clouds are forming out on the horizon, building and blowing our way. The growing wind is whipping up the sea; the waves, now growing higher, can be heard crashing in the cave not far away.

The storm rages until the clouds pass and the wind starts to subside, slowly returning the sea to calmer waters. The sea is still and at peace again.

He tells us to open our eyes.

The teacher now slips a record from its brown paper sleeve, places it gently in position, winds up the handle of the gramophone and unfolds the shining silver arm with a new needle he fitted, taken from a tiny hinged tin.

With his body bent over the gramophone, he carefully places the needle on the outer edge of the revolving record. Then pausing reverently, bent like the vicar giving communion, he gently moves away on tip-toe so as not to disturb the atmosphere as the music starts to play.

I listen in awe.

It's just as he described. I'm there on the sparkling, quiet sea before riding the strengthening waves; my little boat just misses the rocks as the waves rise up, taking me further towards the crashing waves in the cave. They beat the rocks and echo inside the cave. As the black clouds blow over, there's a lull in the wind and my boat becomes steady again. Now I can safely and peacefully sail back to harbour and home.

I want school to end. I want to go straight home and ask for this record. I will never rest till I can hear it again; I want to feel the storm and be near the cave again. I'm inspired by this music. All afternoon I can think of nothing else.

Home at last!

"Please, please, *please*; I need this record. I must hear this music again – *Fingal's Cave* by Mendlesohn."

B52 Responsibility Arrives

Every so often, my mother visits the hairdresser's in Petts Wood to have a perm. On these occasions, she is gone for hours. It's a mystery to me as to why anyone would need to be at the hairdresser's for so long. Luckily she was not in the middle of a perming session when the stair cupboard caught light.

I see a small box standing to one side in the kitchen. She has decided to try a Toni Home Perm. The contents are taken out and arranged in order on the kitchen table. She tells me I am to assist her in the operations as she cannot perm her hair on herself, though I know she puts curlers in her hair at night, covered with a strong hairnet.

The instructions are read. I listen intently. It sounds very interesting but very complicated; so many different waits and washes.

A breakfast bowl has thickish pink liquid poured into it from a small bottle. It has the most unpleasant smell. Thin blue plastic rods, each with an elastic band across to catch the hair, are laid ready for use on the table in a neat row, one under the other like the rungs of a ladder. These items came separately; they were not in the little box. There are enough to form two ladders.

I practise clipping them over and imagine the hair trapped on the little roller. Each will only take a small amount of hair, so that's why there are dozens of them. Also on the table is a little pack of thin papers like dolly's toilet paper.

At grandma's in Bickley, there is toilet paper that feels like these. Its sheets are kept in a cream china container hanging on the wall by the toilet. It allows only one piece to be taken at a time from its letter-box opening; it's uncomfortable paper to use, not soft at all. Upstairs, our Bronco paper (which is very good for tracing) is in a roll; it's the same paper as my grandma's but not cut up into perfect squares and boxed like at Bickley.

My mother goes upstairs to wash her hair; she towels it dry then returns to the kitchen and sits on a stool.

I'm handed a comb with a long spike of a handle. I have to take enough hair to wind around a perming curler; not too much, I'm told, or the rubber band won't close over or might even break. I have to use some cotton wool to smear the wet hair ends with the smelly liquid, then place them in a piece of the tissue folded in half, so as to roll all the ends of the hair onto the thin roller.

I roll up the first one; it's on the very top of her head. The paper is still in place with the hair neatly caught inside.

My mother passes me each paper she's folded as soon as she sees my hand go out ready. The whole task is completed in silence; I need to concentrate. I'm careful not to let the liquid drop or dribble down her face or neck. There's a towel around her shoulders which she grasps to her neck; she's taking no chances.

There are lots of thin blue curlers, so I can use as many as I need; eventually, I manage to curl all the hair on her head. A plastic cap is provided in the box to cover it all. It's a long, slow process, but when the cap is finally in place, I am free to go. I will be called in for the next stage later.

More hair washing has been done. The smell is less now. A different liquid has to be dabbed all over the hair while it is still in the curlers; then another wait. After that, yet another washing.

I'm losing track. No wonder she's at the hairdresser for hours. I'm later called to take the curlers out.

It's quite a moment. Will it have worked? Will the straight hair now be curly?

Such fun. The perm has worked. Each curler has formed the hair into little springs. My job is done; my mother seems pleased.

When will I be asked again? I can't wait; I know I will do a better job next time.

Chapter C The Tents

C1 Holiday Plans

We've got off the train and are here on Waterloo Station, laden with our heavy canvas tents; my mother is clutching the television. The station clock looms high above us.

I'd known little about this approaching trip, except I'd heard the words:

"We're going on holiday; to Hampshire."

It came rather like a Birthday surprise: how exciting!

It's summertime. My father remaining behind to mark papers isn't unusual; the same as when we go to spend holidays at Windyridge.

The television? Where does that fit into this trip?

It's small, chunky and very heavy. The viewing on it is inclined to be *The Brains Trust*, *In Town Tonight*, and "the cricket". Not my mother's choice of watching, I guess; these would be my father's choice of programmes.

My older sister's choice was once *Andy Pandy*, now long outgrown by her. My absolute passion used to be *Muffin the Mule*. Now I like watching, in awe, Jacques Cousteau and his wife Mechela delving into the depths of the oceans. He comes across some amazing sea creatures. My mother's choice of watching, rather than my father's, I think.

Why take the television on holiday? Camping?

I'm curious to know the reason for my mother's struggling with the television, but it's not something I'm going to question. I have learnt to keep my mouth shut when conflicting thoughts enter my head regarding my mother's actions. If I ever try to seek her thoughts, I expect little progress. Best to "keep mum".

We are quite a party standing here, stuff strewn all around us. Mother with three daughters, aged 12, 10 and 8. Plus a television. People pass, glancing at the paraphernalia at our feet. The enormous cathedral-type structure in which I find myself interests me more. The station roof above, its vastness, and the echo of general railway noise. Engines steaming and whistles blowing; mixed up familiar smells of the railway, all, most welcome.

The purposeful way the throng moves from A to B, skirting around us, mostly in hats of some sort: bowlers and cloth caps for the men, felt-brimmed ones for the women – this is what takes my attention; it's a very orderly chaos, one I've not experienced before. I guess it's like this everyday of the week at this time.

We are somewhat out of place amongst this orderly flow of hatted train users.

A man directs a few words towards my mother as he approaches at speed, enough to distract me.

"Where are you going with that?"

His eyes are directed towards the television at my mother's feet.

"Hampshire."

Short and sweet but enough to get an instant reply from the smart-suited gentleman sweeping past:

"It won't work down there."

He's gone, absorbed by the crowd.

Now what? A quick decision by my mother is warranted, which she duly shares with us, no questions asked. It is to stay right here where it is; if it's to be of no use to anyone where we are heading she has no intention of struggling further with the item.

True to her word, we gather the rest of our stuff; we are heading off to another platform to catch the train to Hampshire.

I do wonder who next will lift the television as it sits alone amongst the moving people, all intent on getting to places on their individual agendas.

I doubt that they will be distracted by a lone television in their path. It might sit there for some time. Do they see it with sudden surprise, I wonder? I know I would.

It's not been mentioned again, the television. No regret spoken. The loss has been very quickly dismissed. It feels to me like a strange struggle to have endured when it could be abandoned without ceremony, following a stranger's passing comment.

It was discarded with such ease. Too much ease for me to stop thinking about it; I feel a need to unravel the purpose that prompted the bringing of the television.

I'm definitely not raising the question; my thoughts must remain mine alone.

C2 Garden Arrangement

My mother has rarely taken us on holiday on her own, except to spend weeks at a time at Windyridge. We would be delivered and collected by my father.

Normally, family holidays involve all five of us travelling by car to an area of Britain that holds plenty of historical interest for my father and a farm nearby where we can camp.

This trip has a strange feel about it as we would not normally take our camping stuff by train. The Armstrongs know to expect us. They fit in somewhere to my mother's circle; friends of family rather than relatives, perhaps.

Warsash Court is where we are heading. We are to pitch our tents at the foot of the Armstrongs' very large garden; it's going to be fun. Sleeping under canvas won't be a new experience, but camping in a garden rather than in a field on a farm, will be.

After being greeted by the two elderly sisters, who each have flats in the Court, one up and the other down, they walk with us to the end of the garden from where, they tell us, we will see the sea. It is left to us to decide where we are to camp once we are past a high hedge. We are to settle where the gardener is rarely requested to go. It's an exciting prospect, and I gather we are to be here all summer in what feels like our very own secret garden.

Two tents are put up for sleeping. An extra fly sheet is erected to be used as a shelter for dining and cooking if it's raining. It has no doors or side walls, so it will always remain airy under, yet the ground will remain dry.

We've borrowed a spade to dig a hole for our latrine, which will have a sentry-box-shaped tent erected over it. The door has ties to keep it closed, but I never bother. A visit to this tall, cramped tent is preferably kept to a minimum. It's followed by a ceremonious soil-sprinkling from the earth pile before exiting via the door flap; no hanging about like the guards at their sentry boxes, outside Buckingham Palace.

So now we are sorted, pitched on a sizable strip of rough ground between a tall yew hedge and a boundary of some taller mature trees. The sea is beyond the trees, out of sight except when seen through a gap which the gardeners are instructed to keep open for family viewing of the expanse of water beyond.

C3 She Appears!

"Quick!" A loud, reverberating deep boom is heard not far away. It resounds right through my whole being.

There is one place in this vast garden of Warsash Court where Southampton Water can be viewed. Those of us keen enough, knowing the meaning of the sound, rush to the curved stone bench sited in the gap. It's not many yards from our tents, at the farthest end of the garden.

The area of our camp shielded from the house by the hedge has been allowed, over time, to slip back for nature to enjoy. It is unkempt, but for now, it is our pitch. Water is fetched and a small pit dug for all the kitchen slops. Paraffin and meths are bought for the primus and a line hung between trees for our washing. Our site is completely independent of the residents up at the Court. Perfect.

While seated on this large, solid structure, our view back up to the house is of the deep flower borders stretching up on either side of a wide cobbled walkway. The borders are separated from the path by narrow grass strips, thus keeping the flowers from spilling out over it.

Ladies in crinolines would have walked side by side, merrily chatting as they appeared to slide with tiny steps down to the viewpoint, maybe to look out over and beyond the garden. The curved seat with its curved back is sited proudly as if to say: "Come, sit on me and enjoy the vista."

Young girls too, like me, would have run to the bench whenever they felt their ears vibrating with this glorious sound. They would have run excitedly just as I am doing; me in loose, comfortable clothes, rather dishevelled, they in stiff petticoats and dainty shoes, ringlets in their hair. The boys would have been in stiff, starched collars or more relaxed sailor suits.

For me, the excitement is always the same.

Would small children in the past have climbed up and stood on the seat, craning their necks to see from whence the wonderful sound had come? Perhaps they had no need as the scrub and trees would probably have been kept clear. A band of many gardeners may have been employed to preserve the view of the water, boats and ships. An expansive panorama to be enjoyed by all the visiting promenaders after dining or partaking in afternoon tea.

What an amazing site on which to build a splendid house, with gardens spreading right down to the best view of the sea, close to it yet high up.

No barrier is required to keep marauders out; the land falls away sharply behind the seat. Down, down, down it goes to a path; a path for villagers and workers to pass along close to the shore. Being high above, neither we nor they are in each other's sight. Occasionally, I pick up the noise of passing chat below. This well-constructed stone seat is set in the very best spot on offer; it feels as if it was placed here, with great thought, many moons past.

No longer are the views expansive. I stand high on the bench, bending and twisting to find the gap in the trees that will reveal to me what I long to see: a ship, a liner. Which way to look? Towards Southampton or towards the Isle of Wight? What funnels will she have? Patience is needed. I'm here with it in abundance.

I know I will be rewarded. I've learnt to wait and watch. They are all majestic to me, whichever ship it is that's about to pass.

She noses into view; the wait is finally over. Funnels: one . . .two . . . *three*! Shining red and black.

"It's the *Queen Mary*!"

I want to run and tell the others to come, but I know there's little time. The gap is small.

Serenely she slips by, my eyes unblinking. I stand amazed and full of joy on seeing this iconic liner slide by on the water. I always feel enormously privileged to be camping, just here, so very near to this bench with just enough gap in the trees to see. From where else in the world would I be able to see such a sight?

C4 Messy Fun

Pottery classes are my mother's passion. She talks of whist and chess too, they being part of life at Ash Close; she speaks as if she's left them behind. My passions of Ash Close are long forgotten.

I'm on holiday. I give little thought to home; not much will change there, while we are away. New things arise to crowd my mind and occupy me; there's no space left to think of home once I'm on holiday. There's little to miss except Snowy.

My mother tells us she has plans to acquire some clay tomorrow.

She's discovered a place where some can be retrieved with little effort. The spot is along the banks of the River Hamble. The idea of exploring upriver appeals to me greatly.

Tools are borrowed, trowels and paint scrapers.

With a plastic sheet and a strong bag, we all set off. We pass tidal streams running down to the river. No, it's not here, nor there, so on we go; my mother has a particular place in mind, it seems.

The spot at last. The bank here is thick with luscious, gleaming, silky, grey mud. This is where we stop.

Close to the bank, I dig down a bit. The top layer is too wet and sloppy to collect; the tide has not long left. Lower down, underneath, it's a lot firmer. It looks good. I scoop some out. I don't need much, I'm told. Grey hands squelch the softer mud through my fingers; my hands in a large bowl of clotted cream might equal the experience.

I look a mess; my hands and black wellies are grey with slurry.

We all look a mess!

We roll up our small treasured clay lumps in the plastic and carefully stow them in the bag. Now what?

Back at the tents, we remove our spoils from the plastic and wrap them all in wet tea towels; then we put them back in the plastic. The tea towels are to be re-wetted every so often to keep the clay damp.

Wedging the clay is next: pounding, folding, pushing, much like the baker kneads his dough.

There's more to pot-making than I thought. I am used to the items my mother makes just appearing on the table at Ash Close; proud with glazes gleaming vibrant slip-work patterns.

Any little stones we find in our lumps have to come out. "Foreign bodies" are not good to have in the clay. If I miss a piece of grit, it scratches my hand as I'm working my clay, so I try hard to find them all.

Ready at last; it's passed inspection. Now, can I make something?

I've decided on my pot construction. It's to be a "coiled pot". I'm building mine on my dinner plate; I don't want any foreign bits getting onto it. The plate is round like a potter's wheel, so I place my flat, rolled-out base in the centre. Roll and coil, roll and coil; my clay "string" goes round and round, and my little pot grows taller. I'm told to make sure the joins are tight and well stuck together with slurry. The rolled string's edges dry very quickly.

When did someone first do this, I wonder?

I dampen and smooth out the ridges of the coils enough for them to disappear. I'm impressed; it looks good to me.

More waiting. My pot must not dry out too quickly. First though, I have to knife it off my plate as we have no wire like potters would use or perhaps a dairy that uses cheese-wire to slice up their cheeses.

"Wet one of your hankies so you can keep it covered and damp or else it will crack". I'm definitely going to stop that from happening.

C5 Garden Construction

I've waited days for this next stage: building the kiln. A whole week has passed since we took off up the river.

All items are placed together on a patch of cleared grass out in the open. They are now hard and dry so they can sit straight on the ground without picking up foreign debris.

Slowly and methodically we are to build the kiln around them. Dry twigs have to be gathered, along with plenty of hay-type grass for packing between the twigs.

Our items are well hidden. The kiln is growing.

Damp soil is packed all over — lots of it. It's a mound much like a large mole hill. Finally, cut turf is gently placed all over its surface to finish it off.

We carefully poke holes, low down near the ground. One we stuff with some paper for lighting, placed in not too tightly or it won't stay alight. The opposite holes are to cause a draught for the fire inside to get going. We fetch a pail of water to dampen the roof and walls as it mustn't burn quickly; it's also important to keep as much heat in the kiln as we can. It's looking fine.

The lit kiln is now quiet, with very little smoke and certainly no flames to see. It's warm to touch; a twig is heard, inside, cracking occasionally.

"Just keep sprinkling water; keep it compact so that the heat stays in."

It needs our undivided attention. I'm happy to stand guard and tend to its needs.

C6 Resources Diverted

While sharing the task of tending the kiln, we take it in turns to dampen the top turf to prevent it burning a hole through and letting heat escape.

The mound sleeps but breathes on. It's like a good baby sleeping through the night. A slight whiff of smoke or steam rising lets me know it's still breathing.

Mother did warn us that clay pots, when fired, can explode. I trust it isn't akin to a volcano, about to erupt without warning. I prefer to think of the baby scenario, to that of the volcano.

I am relaxed. Happy to have everything in hand. All pleasantly under control.

I hear an unexpected crackle and glance in a direction, away from the kiln. I'm shocked.

No!

It's the bush. It's on fire within it! We must stop the topiary yew being consumed in flames. I imagine it igniting like a rocket on launch day . . . Whoosh; there'll be no stopping it.

"Mum, Mum! The bush is alight!"

All the water to hand is thrown with great gusto at the bush. How did it happen right over there? So unexpectedly and quickly!

More water is fetched.

Every drop stored near the dining tent is heaved over in an attempt to save the old yew bush.

Such a frenzy.

Great relief − it is enough. The bush is silently steaming. The fire is out.

One side of the bush is now in a sorry state. Peering inside I see a tangle of bush growth, all very black and charred. What will the Armstrong sisters say? My mind is occupied.

Mother doesn't mention the Armstrongs, not even in passing. The state of the old bush doesn't concern her at all as it does me. I might agree that its clipped shape has seen better days, but I'd have hated to see it destroyed through our negligence, before its time.

Amazingly, the kiln is still intact. The baby sleeps. It was not disturbed by the mayhem that descended around it. It slumbered in spite of it all.

We had, so we thought, built it far enough away from the bush.

The fire had crept along deep within the unkempt grass. We had stood close, perhaps on top of it, as it wicked its way along out of our sight.

I think little about the pots after experiencing the near destruction of the topiary.

Fire cannot be predicted, I know that now. It is capable of tricking you and taking you by surprise.

C7 Investigation Deserved

Something unexpected has woken me. Lying here in the tent, I'm feeling confused. What time is it?

I share a tent with my two sisters. It's a twin-poled, heavy, canvas ridge tent, so it's inclined to sag a bit in the middle, depending on the weather. Often at night when rain has fallen, the guy ropes need tightening. We never cause this sag in the canvas; the inclination is for the ropes to stretch in the wet and shrink in the dry.

Now awake, my thoughts are not directed to the dip in the ridge above but to a spectacular glow lighting up the canvas from outside.

My sisters sleep on. I'm lying, contemplating this unusual sight. The tent's canvas is no longer green in the moonlight; it's taken on a beautiful orange hue for some reason.

Sunrise or sunset? When was sunset? When was sunrise? Both could perhaps fit with what I'm observing.

Wide awake, I'm thinking, "Red sky at night, shepherd's delight. Red sky in the morning,shepherds warning." I hope it's sunset.

The glow through the canvas is beautiful. I admire the effect the canvas has on the light, defusing it sufficiently for me not to guess its source. Sunset or sunrise? I conclude the glow is neither as the orange has no sense of having a central source as does the sun at sunrise and sunset.

There's been no change for far too long; it's as if the tent roof will be permanently orange. Why is the colour not fading?

This orange light feels as if it will glow forever; has my world changed while I was sleeping? A UFO perhaps?

I mustn't wake the others, but I have to get up to look. Whatever is causing the glow isn't going away.

I slide up my sleeping bag to a crouch and slowly crawl on hands and knees to the door flaps.

I untie one flap and squeeze out the open half of the entrance.

Out of the tent, letting go of the door flap, I stand up, barefoot in the wet grass.

I'm no wiser, except to know there is no moon and no sun, just wall-to-wall orange of unusual brightness. It is stunning.

I've not been swept up by a UFO. Neither is there one in sight. The wall to wall orange sky is silent.

I turn. The trees look magical; the reflected light is falling on them, turning their trunks, branches, twigs and every leaf deep orange. Beautiful and mesmerising.

The glow seems bright even over towards the gap between the trees. I have to go and look. How far does the orange light stretch — how far out to sea? I'm in no hurry as the glow is constant. It's not like a shooting star: blink and it's gone.

I need my boots, stored under the fly sheet. I must be careful not to touch the canvas; it might alarm my younger sister to see it move, and she might scream, thinking there is an intruder.

I take great care. I need two boots that fit. I don't fancy the idea of going barefoot.

My curiosity is in a hurry, but I've no need to rush as if there's a train to catch. If the sky was changing in the slightest, I would hurry as one does if the sun is about to dip beneath the horizon: there's always a rush then to get the camera out of its case in time. This phenomenon feels stable and continuing. There is no feeling that it will ever change.

Booted, I'm nearing the curved stone seat where the sky's orange extends further. As I climb up, my jaw drops. Jumping off the seat, I rush to the tents to wake everyone.

"Get up! . . . You must see this . . . Mum, *Mum!*"

With all awake, I'm back at the gap, up on the seat, awe-struck.

The oil refinery at Fawley, across on the other shore of Southampton Water, is ablaze! The area is a mass of flame, steady and constant. It's a still night, so the flames all head upwards to the heavens as if ordered to behave themselves. No smoke to hinder the tinting of the cloudless sky to orange. No smell of burning that I can detect.

So not a UFO. Just one hell of a blaze across the water, turning the sky, the sea and all the vegetation orange.

It burns for hour upon hour. Perhaps the thud of an explosion first awoke me in the early hours?

The blaze was spectacular but I find I'm dwelling more on the strange confusion that was set up in my brain; such confusion that I couldn't come up with a sensible explanation.

Investigation outside the tent had been essential for me to reach an explanation. I was prepared to face any adversity, even men from Mars, to get it!

C8 Liberation Experienced

The freedom I've got on this holiday is immense. It's totally different from our other camping holidays when our days have always been mapped out for us: a walk, a castle, a picnic.

This is a different experience: being free to choose without restrictions. To be out with nature with oodles of time to spend looking and studying. Waking up to another day to venture out and explore. Nobody's much interested in what I want to get up to, so I'm left to happily organise myself. I love it.

No "atmospheres" to suffer here. No restraints on what I choose to do in my day. This is the ultimate freedom, which I have never truly experienced before. I could live like this forever.

C9 Content Revealed

Today we are to pull the kiln apart.

Anticipation is soon over; we find very little left that is recognisable. My pot has been swallowed up without any evidence that it ever existed.

I'm not dwelling on this loss; more clay can be fetched, another pot made. The out-of-sight path the fire took to reach the yew bush is what holds my interest. So much to think about. I had been right here as it silently crept all the way to the bush, and it did that right under my nose! If I had been barefoot, perhaps I would have sensed it was happening. I find it quite alarming to think that fire can spread in secret within the grass, undetected.

There's no heat left in the mound. I see clay fragments but no single item to suggest whose bits they are. "Foreign bodies! . . .or perhaps trapped air inside the clay." I was careful to clean my clay, but I wouldn't know about the air that I could have left inside.

"One pot that blows can smash all the others."

I hope it wasn't my pot that did that.

What if we hadn't been near the bush when it caught light? There's no tap down here at the bottom of the garden. A fire engine would have to drive over the lawn and down the wide border of flowers to reach this bush. We were lucky. I'm looking around at all the trees nearby; what if they had caught?

As we rake away the debris, a few bits of pot appear, but I discover that is not all the kiln is offering up.

Charcoal! Lots of it. The thin, black, brittle pieces are all perfect in thickness and length. It appears that the small sticks that were collected to place around the dry grass have been preserved as charcoal. I'll gather it all up and store it safely under the fly sheet.

C10 Welcome Words

I'm down on the shore turning over stones while the tide is low. Further up the River Hamble, the shore can become very thick with mud as the tide recedes, but at the bottom of our road, past the Rising Sun, the shore remains mud free. There's a slipway for launching boats off a trailer; the shore dips more steeply here at the end of the road. The sea is never too far out, even at low tide.

There are the tiniest of crabs under the stones. Sometimes larger ones. Arriving at the shore and glancing across to the water's edge, I never immediately see signs of life; that is under the rocks, waiting for the tide to turn. The creatures I find are never harmed by the weight of the rock, so it's puzzling to know how they can get there when there is so little space.

Once disturbed, they scuttle to the water, with the occasional pause as if they're thinking about their choice of route: "Have I gone wrong?" The pausing is part of their procedure to reach the water safely, which they always do. Their reason to stop appears important, but I don't know why.

They never try to hide on their way to the water; they pass all the stones along the way without pausing. Their direction is towards the safety of the water.

Mother is at the tents, sorting teatime, as it is my younger sister's birthday. Her cake depicts a sailing boat! It was made up at the Court, very cleverly, I think. The two marzipan sails are the perfect colour for a small yacht. I love its blue hull. It's simple but it will be enough to raise a smile on my sister's face when she sees it, I suspect.

My mother makes a brief, unexpected announcement:

"I've enrolled you at the local school in Locks Heath, for the start of the term."

We are going to school in Hampshire!

What an uplifting announcement.

But it's strange that we will be attending school while on holiday.

A "holiday" was not exactly what had been intended then, when my mother walked out of the back door of 6 Ash Close, up through the builder's yard heading for Petts Wood Railway Station. She was not going on a holiday at all; she had decided to leave home!

This time she succeeded.

C11 On Guard

We are washed and kitted out in clean clothes and briefed by my mother to say nothing as to our living situation.

Where do we live? That's not a problem. I will say:

"I live at Warsash Court."

Just remember to miss off "in the garden".

Well, I won't be the one to spill the beans. I love my new life too much to go messing it up.

My younger sister and I catch the double-decker bus for the three-mile journey to start the September school term. I find I'm in Mrs Underwood's class.

Free dinners have been arranged. Won't that cause questions to be asked? It doesn't.

I'm handed the correct dinner money by Mrs Underwood when I arrive on Monday. She tells me I can join the dinner-money queue like all the others and hand it back in.

I knew it to be the same money that was used each week, secretly kept in the corner of her desk drawer.

New friends mustn't be encouraged to pop by; living a bus ride away helps. I can enter the grounds of Warsash Court near the bus stop. There is a solid garden door in the long wall stretching along the pavement. This enters a courtyard. Once though into the courtyard, I'm not in sight of anyone from the road as I walk through the grounds to the tents.

Soon, I hope, I shall become adept at skirting around anyone's curiosity if they hanker to see beyond the door in the wall.

"Authorities" are what concerns my mother, probably. I've no idea what would happen if they found out where we are living. I'm amused by the fact that we are camping but I don't think they would be.

C12 Personal Protection

I'm up and getting ready for school. I'm searching under the flysheet for my bag of charcoal. The whole class can each have a piece. I shan't say, "I found this in our kiln." I shall say, "I found it in the bonfire." I don't want awkward questions to follow.

My mother knows nothing of my charcoal hoard; that it's going to school with me. If I ever find odd or unusual things, they always end up on a teacher's desk. No one around me shows the least interest; a teacher is the next best thing, in my mind.

What I do at school isn't something I talk about to my sisters or my mother. It's my own secret world, and I like it that way.

Any questions my mother might ask I find rather suspicious. She showed no interest when we were living at Ash Close, while I attended Crofton, so I want the same arrangement here. I prefer her lack of interest; it feels safer as I can then be in control of events; make my own decisions.

My mother tells me she once stormed into my father's school, to confront him over something that had annoyed her. To be teaching a class of boys History and for that to suddenly take place! It doesn't bear thinking about.

My mother relates such episodes to me with obvious humour; I'm cringing inside, but do well at hiding it. Contradictions are always best avoided.

I quickly find ways to dodge giving her any information. I want to keep my school hours predictable, now that I have the chance.

C13 Failed Confidence

The double-decker bus heading for Warsash stops just outside the school gate. By the time it arrives, the pavement has virtually emptied; all those walking from school have dispersed; few children end up boarding the bus.

I'm waylaid, distracted by something interesting the teacher is telling me. Realising the time has slipped by, I dash out to catch the bus. I can see its top floor in full view above the well-trimmed, six-foot hedge.

I'm very close, but I can't be seen rushing to catch it.

Through the latched gate, I reach out in time to grab the vertical silver bar to board the bus, but the driver isn't aware of me. Too late; I'm on the ground. My foot didn't quite reach the platform as I pulled myself up . The bus was already moving slowly.

Many films depict the public leaping onto a moving bus, tram or train. They make it look so simple and easy.

I copied the men in the films; it's always men that do the leap, never women. I did the grasp, then the brief run and then the leap, but it didn't work; my raised foot missed the edge of the platform.

I'm in a heap on the ground; the bus is disappearing from sight.

Shocked that I've missed the bus, I am, however, surprisingly thankful the bus driver didn't notice me 'come a cropper'.

Only a brief pause; I need to get to my feet as quickly as possible. I feel very lucky that nobody spotted what just happened. I don't need anybody telling me that it was a stupid thing I just tried. I now know that.

I realise that people doing it in films is not how it is in real life; it's not that easy. Until this moment when I failed, I hadn't appreciated that such an action needs practice.

Brushing the road gravel off, I set about walking home. My being late is not something that will be questioned, as in most families; I've no fear of the alarmost being raised. Sometimes it could feel quite nice to be missed but that's not what I'm hankering for right now.

I can gather my thoughts and relax, on my trek of three miles to home.

I vow never to try that feat again; I realise my legs weren't long enough and maybe never will be. I would never have landed correctly on the platform as the men do in films. At least I know that now; it was my pure good fortune that I didn't come to any serious harm.

"Do not alight when the bus is moving." I've always noted the wording of this plaque screwed securely inside the bus platform. People can read it as they get off or off but I believed it to be an instruction for getting off, not for getting on, also.

"Alight" is not a word I ever hear spoken between people. It's rather archaic sounding. Perhaps the word is meant to work both ways: getting off and getting on?

My lesson today is my secret. It was a salutary one.

C14 Happy Circumstances

October is upon us!

Previously, when we camped on farms, it became a regular occurrence to strike camp and pitch on different ground nearby. It was to help the farmer's meadow grasses recover from the compaction. When we left at the end with everything packed up, the ground always looked much the same as when we arrived.

Nothing like that has been happening on our site here. The grass will be truly flattened, I guess; the grass possibly dead

The weather is cooler. Water, boiled on the primus stove, fills hot water bottles; some chilly nights warrant a hot drink before snuggling down into my sleeping bag. Life is good.

What lies ahead? This isn't a thought that occupies me.

My mother is waiting for a flat in the Court to become vacant. Camping in the garden was always intended to be a temporary measure, I now realise.

It was my luck, I feel, that the delays happened. Life couldn't have worked out better from my perspective. Long may it last, I say; I don't share my thoughts on the matter as I don't think we all see eye to eye on it.

My mother, thank goodness, just gets on with it as if our life is as normal as anyone else's.

I'm enjoying the independent feeling I'm experiencing at Locks Heath Primary. I'm amused by the fact that the headmistress is called Miss Stern. She's elderly and small in stature but can be true to her name. Nobody risks crossing Miss Stern. I'm reminded of the cards from the game of Happy Families. The thought that the pack might include Mr and Mrs Stern and the Stern children makes me laugh.

We have the occasional lesson with the headmistress. This appears to be reliant on her passion for the subject. It is evident that Miss Stern adores Shakespeare, so her passion is pursued resolutely. She also schools us in calligraphy and its presentation which is just up my street.

She has us pick up our chairs and file outside where she arranges all 45 of Mrs Underwood's class in three straight lines backing onto the tall hedge bordering the playground. Tallest at the back.

The first time we were asked to file out, it took me by surprise; I thought we were being arranged for a class photograph.

No camera or instruction to "say cheese"; instead, she held a book in her hand called *A Midsummer Night's Dream*. I was as surprised as Alice, in Wonderland.

All a new world to me, the teacher reading Shakespeare in the playground to juniors, some not able to read properly.

It's rather too cold now for us to sit outside. Hats and coats in the classroom are slowly becoming the norm. The infant class is sizable, with room for a central stoked stove. We have our music lessons there while the infants are somewhere else. These predominantly involve group singing. We all have to perch ourselves on the infants' desks, which aren't much taller than our classroom chairs.

Life under canvas, and Locks Heath School, both have many experiences not to be missed.

C15 Uncovering History

I'm busy weeding the cobbles on the grand path.

I fetched my watercolours out when the borders were full of lupins and delphiniums. It made such a picture looking up the slope of the wide path, narrow grass strips on either side, then each border cascading with wonderful colour. It was straight from a picture book.

The weeds amongst the cobbles weren't as prolific back then as I remember.

I have a feeling of responsibility for the path. Spending those hours on summer days painting the scene has heightened my awareness of the change that has taken place over the months. I don't think I would be doing this otherwise.

It's a long task, but the effect is rewarding enough.

Up nearer the back of the house, I've discovered some wide back steps leading up to French doors that would open outwards onto the garden, just like the ones at the back of Ash Close.

These steps are no longer visible as the growth has completely consumed them. I find clearing them more exhilarating than weeding the cobbles. I have no idea how the steps are constructed; all will be revealed as I scrape away the mat formed by the vegetation. The steps are no longer in use; the path beyond leads only into the wooded area of the grounds.

This is years of growth I'm tackling. With my trowel, old knife and bucket, I could be on an archaeological dig.

I can tell my knife has hit metal. I carefully work around the hardness of the small object. I can tell that it has a shaft, much like a small screwdriver. Perhaps a workman lost it.

A small spoon: a teaspoon! Its shape reminds me of Granny's spoons. This one has no shine; it's seriously tarnished. Looking closely at the back of its shaft, I spot the impression of a lion. It's silver!

What a lucky find.

From my walking in the woods within the grounds over the last five months, I'm familiar with their layout. Clearing these steps has aroused my curiosity as to why, deep in the woods, there is an obvious flight downwards, disappearing into saplings and brambles. I can see the use of the steps leading out from the French doors, but what was the purpose of the other steps among the trees, I wonder?

I've rather assumed they led, perhaps, to the well, serving the community when the Court was the central focus of the village; it later being filled in for safety.

I'm keen to investigate.

They are hard to access as saplings are bent over like crossed swords, baring one's entrance. Peering through I can make out that they lead deep into the earth. Dark, damp; cold and silent. It seems there's no door obstructing the entrance; I creep through, pushing the saplings apart. I've not been asked for the password.

I draw closer to the entrance underground, which I can see vaguely through the brambles now covering the steps. It is well below ground level, with trees and bushes covering the ground above.

With these large, strongly formed steps leading down, it could never have been considered a "secret" place.

What was this place?

The waft of cold air as I enter indicates that it is a fair size, though as yet my eyes have not adjusted to the darkness. Nothing is growing down here as it has above. It feels devoid of nature save for the smell of algae on its wall surfaces., though as yet my eyes have not adjusted properly to the darkness.

Pausing a while, I gingerly take another step inside. It is big! Strange yet not scary; the floor is perfectly flat and even. I discover that it leads nowhere! It is completely empty

The fact that I've found no tunnel at its far end, running under the high wall skirting the garden, is a little disappointing. I liked the idea of a secret way out; not being seen using the door in the wall of the courtyard. What fun that would have been.

Perhaps it has long been blocked up, the tunnel, maybe, still behind the back wall? I feel there has to be a tunnel. What else could this have been for?

The Armstrong sisters provide me with the answer.

An air raid shelter! Fancy that.

Once considered to be a "posh" shelter, compared to others in the village, they were well prepared for bombs to be dropped on Warsash, although we are far from London and the Kent coast.

Nissan huts in Kent look much like large pigsties: cramped, with no room to stand in comfort. They are often used as garden sheds or hen houses. This, on the other hand, is high enough for all to stand. They could have had tables and oil lamps. Chairs, too, and perhaps even beds!

In my mind, I have furnished and decorated the shelter and brought down home comforts.

Did the very large family of the house end up here? Did the sirens sound? It was a lot of unnecessary work to construct it if it was never needed.

I hope that if they did use it, they could continue games of Happy Families or Snakes and Ladders within the safety of its walls.

I take the spoon to the shop up the road in Warsash. Whenever I pass the shop, I look in the window at all the interesting objects. Now I've found the spoon, I have a chance to go inside to ask about it.

He is happy to give me some money for it! I'm more than chuffed that the sisters said I could keep my find.

C16 Nature's Extremes

November is upon us. I'm tucked up in my sleeping bag listening to the howling wind raging through the night. Owls stop hooting, and now all creatures are hunkered down, waiting for the storm to pass.

The wind comes in gusts. Sometimes the tent is still. Then I hear the next gust approach.

Is it squeezing through the gap by the old stone seat? The tent suddenly flaps and billows violently like angry flags wanting to escape their poles.

Crikey! Could the tent take off?

I imagine the wind trying to grab hungrily at whatever it passes; our tent is frustrating its efforts. This wind is bigger than a gale. It's not sounding so happy to just take a few twigs from the trees. Gales are never as strong as this.

I'm lying in the path of a *storm*; a very memorable storm. Yet I feel perfectly safe as long as I lie here.

I've decided it might succeed in taking the tent but it's not going to get me; I'm moulded with the ground and I intend to stay that way until it passes.

The wind seems determined to tug at the tent, but she refuses to be taken. Our pegs are all thick wood, all banged in hard and low with the huge wooden mallet. Not even a force 10 storm could rip them out, surely.

This is what "living weather" feels like. It's unexpectedly, strangely exciting.

A loud crack.

A gun? The noise of wood snapping, followed by the swish of sweeping branches; a hefty thud and the shake of the ground beneath my lilo.

Wow!

I lie listening. I'm very glad it's not raining. If there was rain to match the wind, we would get very wet! A storm without rain? I now know they don't always go together.

Morning has arrived; light is here. It's amazingly still, with birds now singing in the yew hedge by the tent.

I emerge to see a tree stretched out without life, felled by the wind rushing through the gap. A huge tree which had stood proudly, seemingly full of life just one day ago, now lies prostrate. Others remain propped up by their sturdier neighbours.

In my heart, I'm crying for the huge tree close by, knowing that I heard its last moment as it hit the ground. Felled, too late to seek help. Once splendid and standing aloft, it is now a very sad sight.

The huge lawns of the Court are littered with twigs and branches. The grand cedar has a large limb snapped, still hanging.

It was quite something to have felt the power of nature with all her strength yet not to have experienced fear at the time, more a feeling of wonder and exhilaration.

Viewing the tree felled close to our tents and this cedar's huge limb snapped like a matchstick proves it was indeed a force to be reckoned with.

As I was snugly tucked up on the ground feeling no danger, I was like the animal already safely in its den, patiently waiting for the storm to pass and the new day to break.

I emerged with confidence and a heightened awareness that nature's weather is to be experienced. It's not there to be tamed.

It appears that the Armstrong sisters felt the fear last night that was absent in me. Today, the tents are being packed up. The sisters have offered us the disused stable block. Our canvas is to be replaced with bricks and mortar.

Chapter D The Stables

D1 Safe Haven

Moving up into the stable block of Warsash Court sounds pretty romantic to my way of thinking.

I'm helping to strike camp to embark on this new, exciting experience.

Over the last six months, on entering the yard though the gate in the wall, I've passed the stable block scores of times. It was the quickest way to reach the tents at the bottom of the garden.

Never did it cross my mind that I might live in it one day!

Its most notable feature is its huge entrance arch, through which I can see the old stalls where the horses were housed. We are to deposit our camping gear over the threshold in the first stall.

The horses left long ago. The stalls lie empty, the cobbles clean of straw and manure. The inevitable horse smells that would have accompanied it are all gone. The gully drain inside is dry; it's no longer required for washing and sluicing before new straw is strewn and hay-nets hung for each horse.

While relaying the camping gear up the garden, passing the huge limb-torn cedar to reach the stables, I think how much more convenient it will be for catching the bus to school.

Leading off the courtyard is also the back door of the main house. It leads to the Armstrongs' apartments and the laundry area, which my mother is free to use.

Another door off the yard leads into a side flat which is called the Coach House. Possibly it housed a coach and perhaps a governess's cart.

Immediately behind the long back wall of the stable block is a small wood. It carries on further around, skirting the drive which exits onto the back lane, along which we can reach Hook-with-Warsash.

Through the open arch on the left, the stairs begin curving around the walls to reach the upstairs. They are much like ones found in a house, except these treads are in drastic need of attention. It's necessary to step to the sides of some of the treads to avoid the gaping holes created by rot and woodworm. Negotiating the stairs is proving tricky. I'll get used to it, no doubt, as I've found with so many other things. I'm finding I enjoy the unusual aspects of life coming my way, unexpectedly.

Upstairs is one long passage ending in a big room. I expect this was a day-room for the stable lads. The numerous small rooms off the passage would have been where they slept, I guess.

We three are set to sleep in the large room. There'll be plenty of space left for the primus stoves to be set and camping stools positioned for eating.

My mother is to use one of the small rooms and talks of acquiring a divan bed from the Armstrong sisters; it will just about fit in.

It feels like Mother is destined to occupy a "cell", while we three are privileged enough to use the "ballroom".

Life is similar to camping, but indoors. It is less warm, as the trees at the back of the stables keep the sun's rays from warming its walls and the open stairs mean that cold air can find a way up.

The tent, with the door flaps tied, provided good protection; the small canvased space soon warmed up when occupied by our three bodies and three hot water bottles. It was a cosy sleeping place, compared with this vast room. It sounds funny to say that our new abode feels too big when most people would wish it to be larger.

If only I could put the tent up in here; there's more than enough space for it not to be a hindrance. There's no soil to hold the pegs, unfortunately.

I like the thought that in the spring we might need to return to the garden and camp again. I got used to our canvas life with all the routines that were in place to keep things ship-shape. I felt I wanted for nothing; everything was easy, and to hand.

The first and last light of the day finds it hard to penetrate this building, compared to our canvas walls. My days feel immediately shorter than those on the outside because the building is dark inside, most of the time. The large room has high, small windows, mostly clad in ivy.

However, this experience has things to offer that are different from living down the garden.

My mother is nearer the laundry room which includes an ironing board; we are near the dressing-up box, which the Armstrongs keep in the passage. I can drag the box out into the courtyard to rummage through it and see what characters my younger sister and I can become.

I concoct characters for scenes we can act out. Our little plays never have an audience as people rarely pass through the courtyard.

We also have more opportunities to meet up with the "sisters" as we are more likely to pass in the yard. Being invited to play cards more often is a real bonus.

D2 New Playground

My playground now ranges far and wide, from the rocks down on the shore to the old abandoned boats accessible at low tide near the little jetty along Shore Road.

Further up the Hamble river, boats lie resting, snoozing till they can bob again at high tide. By crossing squelching mud, I can see into their bowels.

Along the path, way below the stone seat, heading south towards Hook, huge tree roots now arch high where the many storm tides have swept away the soil. Strong intertwined roots are left exposed under the trunk; it's a strong enough structure to support the huge tree above, much like the intricate rafters of a roof, supporting a huge tower. Underneath the tree makes a wonderful den as there's plenty of room to crawl inside the airy chamber created.

Gulls squawk and squabble for the discarded spoils from small fishing boats. Then, suddenly, all are silenced, interrupted by the reverberating boom that makes my heart leap. I stand, eyes fixed, waiting for a liner to come into view. Maybe she'll be slipping upriver to Southampton Docks. Here she comes: the *United States*! I want to shout from the rooftops: *"Did you see that?"*

D3 Treasured Gesture

Today is Easter Day.

"Come on, let's go!"

I'm calling my younger sister to come downstairs; I'm itching to get started. I have great plans for us today.

The dressing-up box is considered an open invitation. I drag it out from the passage into the courtyard and search through it. I remember seeing curved daggers and black eye-patches. Every child needs a box like this; to me, it is a box of treasures.

Windyridge has a large travelling chest; it still has its sea-travel labels stuck all over. That, too, is stuffed full of dressing-up clothes, together with various bits and bobs such as feather boas and paper parasols from China, brightly painted with huge, exotic flowers. There's also, in Granny's chest, a length of hand-painted silk. Its background is an intense peacock-blue. The paint is stiff and a little cracked but still beautiful.

Today we can become pirates!

Complete with blousy white shirts, thick belts, hats and red-spotted neck-scarves, we don our wellington boots, tucking in our trousers. Wellingtons are essential for crossing squelchy mud. With the tops turned down to show the pale fleecy lining, the black rubber wellies look the part. Hands on the hilts of our wooden daggers now poking through the bottom of our belts, we skip along Shore Road practising our pirate talk, our pirate lilt. It feels like high jinks on Easter Day. Our black hair, we decide, goes well with our outfits.

We haven't yet reached the boat that will become our stage, but it is in sight and the tide is out, luckily.

A large car has pulled up. It isn't from the Court; I don't think the Armstrongs own such a car. Mostly I've seen the two elderly sisters in a Morris Minor. It has varnished wood and two back doors with robust, drop-down handles.

The proportions of this car, however, wouldn't look amiss in the surroundings of the Court. In fact, it would look more fitting in the Court's driveway than here in this neglected, unkempt lane; its body glinting a clean, delicate shade of sky blue, with a shining silver jaguar leaping from the bonnet.

What's this car doing coming down an isolated, unfenced road like this? Not a house for miles, and the incoming tide might even have covered it earlier, further along, leaving a grey potter's slurry on its surface as it receded.

The car's driver is now out, smiling at us broadly. I stand studying the elegance of his motor car. He opens the boot and lifts out two large boxes, one on top of the other. The boxes are brightly decorated, but I can't make out their design. It's a puzzling sight.

"Here, for you girls."

I'm stunned. For us? I'm not asking, just thinking, for all my words have got stuck inside me. I'm flabbergasted because I've just seen a hint of what might be inside the boxes.

He holds them with his arms outstretched so that we can take them. I can see an oval hole cut in the side of the bottom box. Dare I really believe?

We now have them. He didn't stop for a thank you; he just closed the boot and drove on. We are standing here grinning, me holding both boxes one on top of the other.

Easter eggs!

I expected none and neither did my young sister. What great excitement.

This Easter Day is such a special one. We carry home the anonymous gentleman's gift. My plan for the boat can wait; we have something unexpected to concentrate our thoughts on, with good reason to smile a lot.

D4 Desired Items

A van has arrived in the courtyard. Mother's piano is being unloaded!

With great difficulty, it is manhandled out of the van and towards the old stalls beneath where we live.

The two men appear surprised when told that the piano is to be housed in a stall in the stable block, complete with its piano stool.

They stop, rest and chat about the best plan to manoeuvre the piano over the cobbles.

Mother's typewriter is among the items delivered; she displays a sense of great relief to see it. Perhaps it was a special gift at some time in her life.

I know the piano was a twenty-first birthday present from Granny. It's an upright, which is fortuitous, as a grand piano would not have found space in the stables.

Other easier things to manage are unloaded once the piano problem is solved. The Singer sewing machine, my mother's boxed chess set and, I'm pleased to spot my bike secured with ropes to the van's side wall, as are all our bikes.

French polished and gleaming black; any one panel of the piano could double up as a mirror. Its surface is so reflective. In contrast the four cycles stacked alongside look to have 'seen better days'. They will be ridden, and the piano played whenever my mother's mood is conducive.

Did my mother organise the piano's journey here? When she wants something to happen, amazingly it happens, sometimes against all the odds. There's nothing that can stand in her way; nothing is too great to be moved.

My mother is a force to be reckoned with, I've decided.

I'm now thinking back to the television that she abandoned on Waterloo Station.

Did she take it because she considered she could sell it? That she thought it to be the article of greatest value that she could take?

Once she was told her efforts would be useless, leaving it where it stood then became an easy decision. Perhaps her taking it from the house was more to do with how her action would affect my father, she never did enjoy the cricket, as he does.

D5 Back Route

With the arrival of the old typewriter, I see little of my mother, who is now around the stables just for eating and sleeping.

The typewriter is contained in a black box, with a lid which, when folded up and back, cleverly reveals the whole machine ready to lift out. It isn't heavy so is easily carried from place to place.

It is to live for the next few months in a large upstairs room in part of the Court. One of the Armstrong sisters has kindly told my mother she can use her front room to work.

It is a particularly fine and spacious room with a huge bay window giving a view of the garden; the cedar tree is centre stage.

From up here I can glance along the flower beds bordering the grand path, look past the hedge with its arch followed by the burnt yew bush. My eyes can then rest on the stone bench and the sea beyond. There's a great expanse of sea, as I can see over the trees where the tents were and beyond to Calshot Point where a seaplane rests.

It's a strange-looking plane, rather too chunky to take off. Not that it ever does. It's a permanent feature of the landscape. It puzzles me why it is there, apparently with no purpose in life as if it has been on the Point ever since it was born.

I wonder if the Armstrong sisters saw the blaze at Fawley Oil Refinery. I somehow doubt it as they would have needed to be awake in the night. I wish I could have seen the sky and sea from here. Was it orange right across to the Isle of Wight? I'm trying to imagine seeing it from this window, the Needles aglow, rising from an orange sea.

The blaze was nearer to us than here, but there's far more sky and sea on view from this window.

On weekends when I visit, I can see many small boats scurrying around buoys, attempting to win races. Hamble has lots of sailing clubs, all with weekend events. The sea is then awash with them, all dwarfed by any liners heading into or out of Southampton Waters passing the Isle of Wight and heading out across the Atlantic to America.

If I happen to be in this room when a liner passes, I am allowed to use the big telescope which stands by the large, low window. The boom of the liner does not resound in me in the same way up here; the sight of the passing ship is not nearly as exciting, yet I can view it for far longer than I could at the gap.

Being closer and seeing it briefly held more exhilaration for me than being here with a good view. I feel strangely distanced from the experience I used to have of the liner when I was on the seat.

Here there is no high expectation, no immediacy of time being precious, that it will soon run out.

Down at the gap, there was no time to waste idly blinking or chatting as if time was of no importance. Having the brief moment to view was immeasurably more memorable than the expansion of time now offered in this apartment.

Through the telescope, it's more like I'm watching a film. I preferred the stone seat; the small gap with the breeze on my face. I never let on to the Armstrongs how I think; it could sound ungrateful. The use of the telescope is considered a privilege.

The room is furnished very comfortably. Persian rugs of different sizes cover parts of the oak floor.

My mother sits at a large gateleg table on which her typewriter is always placed.

To reach this fine drawing room, I have to go through the door in the yard, pass along tight corridors and through another door, which immediately leads up a long, windowless flight of stairs; electric lights are left on all the time.

The final small, plain door at the top of the uncarpeted stairway is like entering a broom cupboard.

Alice in Wonderland could have opened this door to see the extraordinary sight of the Mad Hatter serving jam and cream scones on a silver platter to the Queen of Hearts.

It's not often I go up.

My mother prefers the room to be left to her for thinking alone with no disturbance, so I keep my visits rare.

The usual daily things get done, but most of my mother's time is spent typing. It feels as if she will go on forever writing her "statements".

"I'm writing statements today. Get yourself a sandwich."

The other new word that's now entered my vocabulary is "respondent". Our birthdays are greeted with:

"I don't suppose the respondent will remember your birthday."

Writing down what caused her to leave my father occupies her day in and day out. I hear regularly of the respondent, statements, cruelty, courts, custody and the judge.

Her filing for a divorce doesn't stop my flow of life; that carries on regardless.

D6 Unusual Decision

Negotiating the stairs is quite an art. The middle parts of some of the remaining treads are no longer safe. 0I read a message in here somewhere: "Use the innocent-looking treads at your peril!"

Over the months, I've become amazingly adept at climbing both up and down as if nothing is amiss. None of us has come to harm.

In the days when the stairs were in better order, one of the young, sprightly-keen stable lads might have been called down to assist on the master's unscheduled return. His horse would need to be unbridled and brushed down before it could settle into its well-earned net of hay. The other horses would shift in their stalls on hearing the clatter of the master's horse's hooves on the cobbles. Perhaps some of the horses were those of guests invited to the Court?

This building is of the past, not the present. Long ago, it moved into disrepair and then dereliction, but now it is loved — by me. It is home.

Instead of hooves on the cobbles, it's the notes of Beethoven's *Fur Elise* echoing up the stairs and filling the courtyard.

It's unusual for me to feel sick. On this very rare occasion, I'm not my usual self.

All night I've complained of tummy pains. Sitting on the large galvanised "poo" bucket in the passage overlooking the courtyard solves nothing; there's merely more groaning as my pain worsens with moving. It's proved each time to be a fruitless exercise and still is, one I'd sooner not do, but my mother keeps insisting.

Now dawn is breaking. The light from outside is seeping through the unwashed windows of our room; the bird song in the wood behind the stable block is growing with intensity as more and more birds join the chorus. My mother concludes:

"You're not fit for school."

I've been moved from my lilo and sleeping bag in the large room to my mother's bed. It's a single divan, but it still takes up over half of the stable lad's allocated space.

I'm now alone, feeling quite privileged to have a bed to lie in with sheets, woolly blankets and an eiderdown. Now I have the block all to myself I can enjoy the peace and relaxation; by lying still, I have no pain bothering me.

Being in a soft bed feels strange after ten months of sleeping on my lilo which on numerous occasions loses air. My new situation reminds me of the story of *The Princess and the Pea*. Even if I was a princess, I wouldn't complain about a pea being under this mattress. Anyway, there are no more mattresses in the stables, so there'd be no point in asking for another. I'd have to put up with the feel of the pea. My morals would be different from the one intended: "Don't ask for the impossible."

I loved *Aesop's Fables* more than Hans Christian Andersen's *Fairy Tales:* the Lion set free by the Mouse who gnawed through the hunter's net that held him, and the Crow who dropped stones in the pitcher to reach the small amount of water to drink at the bottom. The moral given in my book was to always think through a problem, but I think it was more to do with not giving up.

My sisters have left for school; my mother rode off long ago on her bicycle. She rides her bicycle some distance to a private boys' school where she has a job as an assistant cook. My mother always has to take off the earliest.

While I'm lying still in bed, my thoughts are interrupted. A doctor is talking to me. Where did he spring from?

Golly gosh; I'm mighty impressed that he risked life and limb on the stairs. He's standing here by my mother's bed as if he's been puffed in by the rubbing of a genie's lamp.

D7 Memorable Attention

I was happily lost in my thoughts until the doctor appeared.

There's no door to be knocked on or a bell to be pulled. It isn't a question of having "an open door"; there isn't one.

A few questions and a few deep prods to my stomach, causing me to yelp like an injured dog, have prompted the emphatic diagnosis of: "acute appendicitis", rather than a rumbling one.

My mother had been a nurse at Guys Hospital before the war, together with her older sister Josephine. Had my mother known what was wrong with me? Is that why she decided to send for a doctor? She'd not mentioned doing so, before she left for work.

I know of this illness. My mother's sister died from peritonitis not so long ago. Her problem had been caused by a ruptured appendix. The signs of appendicitis came too late.

Living in isolated Scotland, on a farm in Dumfries, had not been the best location to have acute appendicitis, I guess. A delay in the arrival of the ambulance would have been inevitable.

She left behind my two cousins. My aunty Josephine's sudden death, some years ago, had been a great loss to my mother.

There is a photograph of my mother and her sister Josephine in their nurse's uniforms standing outside Guys Hospital. It sits on Granny's bedroom chest-of-draws. That was how I first knew that my mother was once a nurse.

The doctor instructs me to lie still until the ambulance arrives.

He's left.

My thoughts have switched to the unexpected experience I will have of seeing inside an ambulance.

My mother's tiny room has a small window high up, but little light penetrates; the window is ivy-clad. The woods are not accessible from the courtyard, otherwise I would have explored them.

A large, uniformed man is silhouetted at the door; his outstretched arms are scooping me up and out of bed. He proceeds to carry me to the precarious stairs.

The windows in the passage over the courtyard show daylight now; occasionally there's moonlight, like last night. The stairs, on the other hand, are always dark, day or night

I know the hazard he is to face negotiating them, but I feel safe, cherished; in no way am I nervous as he searches with his feet in the dark to find the stronger sides of the treads. I remain quiet and relaxed.

I say nothing. I'm enjoying being cradled with care.

Right up until he places me on the bed inside the ambulance, I've been in a world I have rarely experienced. The feeling came, surprisingly, from the tender security of this stranger's arms.

It isn't like I ever craved or expected such a feeling from either of my parents or their parents; I haven't.

Negotiating the stairs was a big event, but I trusted the arms that carried me. I felt safe while on my way down to the outside world. It was without hindrance or mishap: an especially good moment for me.

It was not sought or planned today. It just happened. Circumstances brought it about, nothing more.

I loved the moment. It is over; I move on to other thoughts.

Travelling from Warsash is not without pain. I feel every bump. But eventually the ambulance arrives. Where are we? I have no idea. The journey was spent lying on my back, so I saw nothing.

"This is Southampton Children's Hospital."

The upstairs ward is huge. Children well spaced, all neatly in bed. I, too, can lie quietly and pain free as long as I'm not disturbed by movement. Little noise is heard, only the clattering of a trolley with its metal equipment.

A new world, far removed from whence I came today, to be sure. There is much to marvel at, and I will certainly have plenty of time for that. I'm here for ten days.

D8 Sustenance Required

I lie very still in the hospital bed. This way I can keep the pain away.

The high, very large metal bed is cream, with white cotton sheets, thick and heavy. Few words are spoken. When I was put into the bed, however, the nurse had smiled, saying:

"I'm your namesake. I'm Fran too."

I warmed to her straight away.

It isn't she, now, pushing the food trolley past the bottom of my bed without as much as a glance. Twice now the trolley has stopped at the bed to my right, first lunch, now tea.

I'm glaring at it as, in disbelief, I watch it sliding across from my right to my left without so much as a moment's pause, my hopes of something to eat or even drink dashed.

For my own sake, I'm not moving a muscle, so is it possible that she hasn't spotted me? The beds are huge, and I am small.

I've noticed that not all the beds are occupied. They are well spaced out in the large ward, so perhaps this to her is another empty bed. It certainly feels like that is the case. Her passing me by isn't that she is deliberately ignoring me.

I hear the rattle of the trolley in the corridor outside. The double doors are held back. It could be bedpans.

Now, through the door, I can see that it's food. This time I will have the courage to speak; I will make sure the lady sees me lying here. It's now or never; nighttime darkness is descending. I must speak quickly before she's reached the end of my bed in case the trolley is on automatic control.

"Do I get any food?"

"No, I'm afraid not. It will make you sick."

Make me sick? I don't think so; food never makes me sick. I love all kinds of food. I've never in my life refused food, and it has never made me sick!

The trolley has rattled past and reached the next bed.

My courage is growing. I will try for water next time anyone passes. At least that lady had a voice. Asking for food didn't work. I will try water.

"It will make you sick."

I don't believe it. Water never makes anyone sick. It's rubbish saying that to me. I'm not "taking it lying down" as Mother would say.

"No, it won't."

The nurse assures me it will. How can she say that?

Parents tell their children: "Say the magic word."

I will plead with the most pleading tone I can muster.

Screwing up my face and stretching my cheeks, my eyes like those of a dog wanting his master to throw the stick, I'm poised and speak the one and only "magic" word:

"Pleeeee . . . ze."

"Only little sips then."

Wow! The water is fetched, along with a banana-shaped metal dish which she now holds under my chin. I now believe that she believes I *will* be sick.

I make sure my sips are the very smallest possible. I'm determined, after all my efforts to achieve this special moment, that I'll not be needing the dish. Water will never make *me* sick.

Thirst is no longer of importance to me. Not being sick is on my mind.

I've rarely felt as if I'm going to vomit; I don't feel like it now, so what harm can water do to me? It makes no sense at all.

I'm very happy now that I've proved water does not make *me* sick!

D9 Missed Opportunity

"You will have your operation early tomorrow morning."

Food soon after, I hope. I'm not thinking about the operation one bit, but rather of the food I will then be able to relish.

Nobody told me that I would have to miss all my meals before the operation, or that the operation wouldn't be done immediately. "Acute appendicitis," the doctor had announced. It's not an emergency after all, then?

The breakfast trolley now trundles past, not stopping. My last food was back at the stable block: neck of mutton with pearl barley, cooked up on the primus stove. It's been so long I've lost track.

Now, at 11 o'clock this morning, I'm wheeled out through the doors. I've been gowned up ready since sunrise. I got the same answer every time I enquired, which was often.

"He hasn't arrived yet."

I'm now on the move. Not me personally; it's my bed that is on the move through the double doors heading for the theatre.

Through another set of doors, I find I've been pushed into quite a confined area; the doors to the theatre are behind me, I'm told. I'm interested in what the theatre will look like. There is no daylight here; perhaps we are underground. It has that kind of feeling.

With the bed now stationary in the "tunnel", my hand is lifted. I hear these few words then feel the faintest prick on the back of my hand:

"You will just feel a little prick."

I'm back in the ward with nothing changed. The prick in the back of my hand could have passed unnoticed, but I'm glad to have known that was the moment I would see no more, feel no more; I know that was the moment I was cheated of my look into the theatre.

The prick worked before another thought could enter my head.

If only they could have waited till I was through the next doors before pricking my hand. I was so looking forward to seeing the theatre.

D10 Forging Adjustments

My recovery brings with it lots of checks and questions. Instructions too and the regular reading of a board hung on the end of the bed.

Confined to bed; it's a strange life. I feel in my mind that I could get out of bed and run around. A few children are at the tables in the centre of the ward doing activities. It's too far for me to see; I wonder what they are doing?

A nurse carries an oblong box. It's coming my way. All done up in brown paper and string.

I cannot believe it is for me.

Delight! I recognise Aunty Jean's writing; it's from Windyridge!

Stems, wrapped carefully in damp cotton wool; a fine garland of syringa, daisies, clarkia, dog-rose and apple blossom, all collected from Windyridge garden.

I could never have dreamt that a parcel could contain such wonder; that live flowers could arrive all the way from Kent, by post.

Nurse Fran is coming over; she asks me if there's anything I would like. I doubt if she can help.

I find I'm asking anyway:

"Some fresh air?"

I miss the fresh air so much.

With that, the fresh air is arranged. My bed has its brakes released and I'm wheeled out through large doors onto a long veranda. The wall on my side of the room with high-up windows has been obscuring this amazing outdoor space. Others have their beds pushed out to join me.

Heaven has definitely arrived. The sun on my face and a breeze in my hair. I hope Nurse Fran asks me again if there is anything I would like. I know exactly what I will say:

"My hair washed, please."

So here I am, Nurse Helen washing my hair over the small basin at the far end of the ward.

Bliss.

From no food to this: hand-picked flowers from Windyridge, fresh air and a clean head of hair.

I won't want to leave.

D11 Observing Incomers

Visitors are allowed at certain times of the day. However, I know from the distance of the ambulance journey that

I am now a long way from Warsash, so I don't expect visitors.

Filing in, as if they've been queueing behind locked doors at the "sales", they know exactly which "department" they are seeking. Nobody seems at a loss as to where to head, yet all the patients in here must look much the same, being small people in big beds. No mistakes are made.

Nurses carrying things in both arms push the double doors open with their bottoms. They come through backwards, then the doors spring shut. I have plenty of time to observe all that goes on. The doors are not locked; visitors dutifully queue till "opening time".

Those visitors that arrive late have less time; the hand bell is rung at closing time when the ward quickly clears of all visitors.

The bell sits on the matron's desk, but it's not she who has the responsibility of using it. It's not picked up at any other time. It's rung in a visiting ritual that maintains a predictable atmosphere.

With each bed having plenty of space; any talking or chatting is out of earshot of next-door patients. It feels very subdued. Numbers at each bed appear to be strictly controlled.

Semi-recumbent, I'm propped up with the same regular pattern of pillows, so I can see all around. Visiting time is always an interesting interlude for me, one that I'm ready to embrace as I know exactly when it will occur and finish.

Nurses are astute; I begin to feel my four pillows need puffing up so I can see better around the room. As if by telepathy, a nurse comes over to do this very thing for me during visiting hour. The pillows are all removed while I lean forward, then puffed up and replaced in the same special pattern. Another nurse then comes over to assist.

Both together, their arms slide under my armpits and I rise up to rest against the newly puffed-up pillow arrangement so it hugs my body, supporting me.

By the time I leave here, I will know how to do this clever pillow arrangement for sick people and also how to do "hospital corners".

D12 Problem Solving

I'm not allowed to get out of the bed.

I'm washed where I lie. It's quite an art form completed by one nurse. She rolls me onto my side. With a towel stuffed along my back to keep the bed dry, she washes the whole of the exposed half, then rolls me to face the opposite direction and washes the remaining half. She's behind me with a bowl of water, sloshing occasionally. This operation is called a bed bath.

Heavy metal bedpans stacked on a trolley are pushed around at certain times. One is slid under each bottom, under the blankets.

When the nurse comes to take mine, she sees it's empty. The nearby sink tap is turned on fully. No word is spoken. The nurse then collects the other pans, stacking them back on the trolley. It's all done with great speed as if a clock is ticking, ready for "Time up! Come in number 5."

Returning, the tap is turned off. She removes my pan, assuming it's been used.

I see her face full of concern.

What is clear to me is not to her, I'm thinking.

"I can't use the bedpan if my legs are lying out in front of me in the bed; it feels like I will miss the pan and wet the bed. I know if I hang my legs over the bed while sitting on the pan, I will be able to do it."

Breaking the rules? Will it be allowed?

The nurse listens; my requested position, surprisingly, is applied. The problem is solved. The running tap was never going to fix my issue; just a chat about the problem was all that was needed, in my case.

D13 Suitably Enclosed

I eat whatever is put before me; I'm not a fussy eater. At intervals, the board clipped on the end of my bed is lifted, scribbled on and replaced.

This time, the board is lifted, studied and put back; no scribbling. The rhythm has been disturbed, but I can't guess why.

Screens are rattling across the floor on their tiny wheels to be placed around a bed in the ward. This is quite a regular occurrence. Secret things go on when a bed is enclosed with blue curtains; I've no idea what.

Often, after a very short time, the screens are folded and rattle back to where they came from.

The rattling is stopping near my bed. If they get pulled around me, I will at last know what goes on in secret as I will be the one enclosed; the mystery will be solved.

The screens are now around my bed, closely arranged so that there are no gaps for others to look through. One section acts like a door. The gathered cloth of the screens, in matching blue, is fixed like curtains up and down. I'm asked how I feel; I quickly answer:

"I feel fine."

I'm asked to roll on my side with my back towards anyone now standing within the curtains; how odd to position me so that I can't see what they are doing.

"We need to look in your bottom."

I'm trying hard to imagine what that means; how can anyone look in my bottom? It's not possible.

I don't think for long. A finger is now up there, moving around.

I wasn't worried, but it took me completely by surprise. I can see the point of the screens now.

At home, if I don't go "number two", this investigation certainly never happens. Nobody's put a finger up my bottom before! After answering "no" to my mother's question "Have you been number two?" a bottle is fetched from the medicine cupboard in the bathroom. I'm dosed regularly with the stuff at home.

In here, if I've not done "number two", I'm not asked. Nurses look at a chart on a board at the end of the bed.

I'm struggling to work out how sticking a finger up will help. All that's needed is a spoonful from the special bottle.

D14 Embarrassed Encounter

"Ding-ding"; the bell rings. All the visitors head out, waving back into the ward.

As I watch them leaving, I observe a lady coming in. Summer coated, hatted with white gloves, so not a nurse; if a visitor, she is far too late, I'm certain of that.

I fear she is heading my way. If she really is coming to me, she will have to walk halfway down the ward to where my bed is, on the left. She's striding this way with no hesitation; with intent, just like all the other visitors I've observed. This lone figure – who is it?

I feel embarrassed; I'm speechless. It's my teacher from Locks Heath: Mrs Underwood. It's like a visit from the Queen: the coat, the hat and the white gloves. My heart is beating fast and I find it hard to speak. I'm unnerved and well out of my comfort zone. I want a hole in the bed to magically swallow me up.

"I'm very happy, thank you."

"The food is nice."

"I like it here."

What if she asks me if I miss my family? And talks about "home"? I want her to go. I feel cornered; trapped and very uncomfortable.

Where might the conversation lead? It's awful. "Please go" is all I can think of. I'm willing her to turn and leave. I want no more questions for fear of inadvertently "spilling the beans".

"Well, we all look forward to you joining us back in class very soon."

I'm relieved that it's over. I felt overwhelmed by wanting to be saved from her possible questions. I wanted to run, but I couldn't. I don't want that feeling again.

Time now to recover from my ordeal, relax and settle back to enjoying my stay here.

"That was nice to get a visitor." A glass of water is placed on the side table for me. The nurse doesn't expect an answer, thank goodness.

I'm not missing anyone; I don't need any visitors.

I feel bad that my teacher came all that way to visit me; I had so little to say. I couldn't help myself; it wasn't that I was ungrateful.

I was taken by surprise without time to prepare myself. I have secrets I must keep; that was the problem.

Unexpected questions from unexpected visitors create a nightmare in my brain: how can I answer? What can I answer?

D15 Emotional Turmoil

My memorable stay in Southampton Hospital will soon be coming to an end. My only ordeal has been the visit from my teacher. I'm very glad that it hasn't been repeated.

I do have a puzzle, though: the nurses have become very insistent:

"Never get out of bed on your own."

It's not something I would do without permission.

It's very strange: I've never needed help to walk, so why are they saying this?

When I arrived, the nurse said I would be sick if she gave me water. Now I'm told I can't walk on my own, that I will have to learn again.

"You won't be able to stand."

I don't believe that I could forget how to walk. I will do as I'm told, but when I'm allowed out of bed, I will show everyone that I haven't forgotten! I sipped water and wasn't sick; it wasn't hard as I didn't feel sick.

I'm thinking about all the strange talk that's spoken in here, wondering how it comes about. I'm curious to know; there has to be a reason behind it.

The swing doors have opened. I stare in disbelief. It's my father!

Panic.

My heart is beating in my chest. I'm not in control; the blood is draining from my face.

A bombshell. Why is he here?

My father is striding across the ward towards my bed.

I don't hesitate. I roll over, leaving my back to greet him. I don't want to speak. I have nothing to say. What I say won't sound right or make any sense to him.

Best not to speak when my brain is in such turmoil.

Coaxing doesn't work. My ears are closed to all sounds. My father waits, but he's wasting his time on me.

"Your father's gone."

Relief; my worst moment is over. I wish I had known that I could be put in such a position; nobody told me that my father might visit.

I responded in the only way I could for fear of saying something I shouldn't. If my father was here to ask me questions, how was I to answer? Where would my answers lead? It was too risky; I had no trust that my answers would bring any good; maybe they would bring harm.

My parents don't know how I think or how I feel.

There's never been talking amongst us for them to know what I'm like or how I am.

I've always been in my own "mind-world" and happy in it, working things out on my own.

Family provides me with a roof to keep me dry and they feed me.

I've had good practice creating my own interests. I enjoy life.

With my parents now apart and me no longer living in a predictable world, life has become an unplanned, uncertain journey. I'm not drawn to live with anyone in particular. If I was told to now live in this hospital, it would feel fine. It's dry and there's food.

I want to go back to the stables, the garden, the freedom and the fresh air, but it's not a feeling to be with my family.

I could never speak this out loud.

I've learnt how I feel by being in this hospital: there's nobody I need back home; it's other things that inspire me to leave.

D16 Unexpected Difficulty

Did my mother contact my father and tell him where I was? I'm stunned that she could do that to me.

She dislikes my father so much and wants us all to feel as she does. It never crossed my mind that she would tell him where I was. Why did she "sell me down the river" like that?

Today I'm to have walking practice! No more bedpans. They're an ordeal I can well do without.

Nurses on either side are supporting me under my armpits as I slide down off the side of the bed to feel my feet on the floor.

Wow! Who would have thought I could feel like a drunken man?

I'm not in any pain. My cut is well healed and the stitches removed, which was of great interest. It's never been painful having stitches removed; I find it surprising, a tugging feeling, that's all.

"We did tell you that you would have to learn to walk again."

What has happened? I accept what they say.

"In a few days, you'll be walking again on your own; all will feel normal. Then you will be able to go home."

D17 Destination Change

It's time to leave Nurse Fran after my ten-day stay on the upper floor of Southampton Children's Hospital. I leave with the few things I had when I arrived, plus a small box holding my stitches.

I was offered them, so l feel they are something I'm meant to treasure.

I'm instructed on what I must avoid doing when I get home:

"Take things easy. No games or lifting for a while."

I'm not at all nervous about the cut this time as I can see that it has healed. When my cut foot was stitched, I couldn't see it, so I had no idea how quickly it had sealed over.

Next stop: Warsash Court — the stables, fresh air, the garden, school and normal life again. I'm soon to be on my way!

I climb enthusiastically into the transport, and we set off down the road.

"You are first going to spend some time convalescing."

I'm dazed. I'm not going home? Convalescing? Recovering? None of it makes any sense. I feel quite well; I am already recovered. I don't need more time. I'm upset and feel cheated. They had said:

"You'll be leaving us tomorrow to go home. You've done really well."

Who knew this plan was in store for me? Who made it?

Having arrived at the place where I'm to "convalesce", my transport pulls into the drive of a forbidding-looking house closely surrounded by tall trees and bushes. I've no idea where we are.

Around the front of the building, a huge porch, big enough to sleep in with a proper bed, looms into view. It has a castle-like solid oak door.

Inside the house is dark, as the only daylight finding its way in is from the open doors of the rooms off the big hallway where wide oak treads of a staircase stretch upwards.

They bend round so I cannot make out how high they go. It's a place belonging to long ago, when it would have had huge inglenook fireplaces you could walk into and sit in, vast kitchens in the basement, then in the drawing room while playing cards, thick, long cords you'd pull to summon servants to bring afternoon tea, or calling from your boudoir for warm water to fill your washbowl in the morning.

A place built big enough to house a large family and all its servants.

D18 Expressed Displeasure

After the greeting, I'm shown to a room on the right, just past the bottom of the uncarpeted staircase with its great posts on either side that are far taller than me.

The heavy door opens into a huge, tall-ceilinged room with a dozen or so beds round the sides. Several tables are clustered in the centre. They have a mixture of things on them: books, pencil cases, some boxes and larger tins.

Two sides of the room have very large bay windows reaching high up to the ceiling. There's room in each bay for two beds side by side. The room should be lighter, but the trees in the garden hang their branches close. The dark oak-panelled walls overwhelm the beds. They all look very small after the high, large beds at the hospital. How different this is.

These beds will be easy to get in and out of, though. I will be able to sit on the side and my feet will touch the floor. I'm directed to one in the alcove of the huge bay window on the right. There is little to see out of the window except, maybe, the odd car or van pulling up.

Nobody stays in bed. I can't tell whether anyone is sick or even why they are here. They take pills and mixtures. T.B. and diabetes I hear mentioned. I have no illness and I take no medicine. I feel I don't fit in here.

What is worse is that I don't know how long I will be here. My mind will find it hard to settle. I feel I can't settle if I'm never told anything. I long to be standing looking out to sea on the garden bench at Warsash Court.

Nobody tells me when I will be free.

My world has become just this one room. Nobody who sleeps here needs to go anywhere except when a relative arrives to visit; only then do they leave the room. Visitors do not enter this room. It appears out of bounds, which feels a strange way to be; it's so unlike my hospital experience.

Nobody is unkind; they all look happy. It's only me that wants to leave. If only I could have stayed longer in Southampton where I was happy.

I hear that this place is in Bursledon.

I know there are boat yards and boat builders here because I passed some when we were close to arriving, but I don't know where Bursledon is. It must have a river nearby if boats are made here. We passed through no village or hamlet when arriving.

The days pass. I feel no better about being sent here.

"Your dad is here."

I'm prepared this time.

I prepare my mind. I'm not going to hide how I feel this time. I know what I want.

We walk briefly in the garden under the trees. We don't walk far or for long as it's a small area. There's no joy for me, even though I'm outside at last; my mind is focused on getting my message across while I have the chance.

My father must tell my mother that I want to leave so that she can come and fetch me. I know that they are in touch with one another, now.

I return to the room holding a small box of sweets.

The unopened box is taken from me, and before my eyes, the sweets are emptied into a tin which sits on the centre table.

"It's a tin so everyone can share."

I should have opened them out in the garden.

I shall soon forget about the loss of the sweets as I'm certain I will be collected and taken home soon. My father, I trust, will pass on my message to my mother.

No change. More days pass in Bursledon. Did my parents speak to each other? What are they doing to help me? I never get a single sweet from the tin.

The day has finally arrived! I'm going back to Warsash Court: the garden space, with its grand flower borders, cedar tree and topiary yew. The stables! I will run over every inch, shouting:

"I'm back!"

Chapter E The Flat

E1 Making Adjustments

It's a great feeling to be back at Warsash Court, but I find I'm no longer having to carefully watch any stair treads.We now live in the single-storey flat across the courtyard: the Coach House.

The couple living there kindly brought forward their date for moving into the pub they are renovating so that I could come home.

It is now clear to me what the Bursledon "convalescing" was about. It wasn't that I needed to convalesce; it was the authorities not allowing me to come home to live at the stables. I wish someone had told me;

The stables were not any bother to me; nor were the six months of camping, but I always knew the authorities would make a song and dance if ever they found out how we were living. My mother has never shown concern about repercussions that might occur except how we look when going to school; I'm always dressed looking tidy and clean; that area of our lives has always seemed important to her. I think it's so no questions are raised, it doesn't arouse curiosity if we are decently turned out.

The doctor would have reported it, I suppose. Such a fuss about nothing; none of us fell ill until my appendicitis. Both my parents have had their appendixes removed, so I don't think it was living conditions that caused it, even though the doctor said that it may have been the result of bits of grass in my food during the many months of camping. I never had reason to see a doctor during our camping months; before that I had numerous visits for one reason or another. Camping was good for me, I think.

Now there's no more need for the primus, nor carrying up our water and the daily emptying of the "night soil" from the galvanised bucket into the manhole in the yard. We have water taps at a sink and a toilet!

Here in the flat we also have furniture, beds, a stove and a hoover for the rugs that are dotted about the flat. Everything we will ever need is here.

The flat is squeezed between the road and the main house. It has no inside connecting door to the Court; it is "self-contained" unlike the other flats here. Other occupants have to enter the main house to reach theirs.

I can't help a broad grin stretching across my face as I enter the comfortable sitting room; my eyes are transfixed. I'm looking straight ahead through glazed French doors; the steps I painstakingly cleared some months ago lie just beyond! Life never ceases to amaze me; I had, unwittingly, been clearing our own steps.

I share a small bedroom; its outside wall backs onto the pavement and continues to the blue door that enters the courtyard from the road.

The window is too high to see out; I would have to stand on my bed to reach up to the sill. I can clearly hear people chatting as they pass in the street.

I haven't worked out why I can hear them but I don't think they can hear me when I chat to my young sister.

E2 Provided Essentials

I'm so pleased to be enrolled in the Brownies again.

I can reach the hall by myself as it's in the village. Parades take place in a church some miles away, so I may have to miss those.

I iron my yellow tie and fold it in a special way before putting it round my neck; we have an iron here in the flat and a fold-up wooden ironing board with an asbestos section for the hot iron to rest upon, face down. It can't burn through this special material, no matter how hot the iron becomes, yet it will soon scorch the ironing board cover if it's left there by mistake. It's easy to get distracted.

These laundering items are provided for whoever rents the flat, same as the New World cooker and the Hoover.

E3 Invited Guest

My aunty Jean has come to stay. She also knows the Armstrong sisters. Perhaps the Armstrongs know Granny and that is why we were welcome to camp in the garden for all those months. There can't be many places where one could do that.

Her stay isn't to be short; she's taken a job just down the road near the shore. I can visit Aunty Jean where she works at The Crab and Lobster. It's down past the Rising Sun.

As I round the corner by the pub, I glance up at the sign of a bold blazing sun, stuck out at an angle from the building. You can't miss it as it is silhouetted against the sky over the shore.

My aunt works at the back of the restaurant; she deals with the live lobsters which she fetches from a huge, high tank outside in the yard. They are very much alive. She needs to hold them firmly across their backs to avoid their moving limbs and huge pincers.

The next bit about her job I hate. I'm surprised that my aunt can work here.

I leave and can't bring myself to visit again. I will never go there to work, I know that.

My mother also works near the shore, but further up the Hamble River past the Crab and Lobster. She's in a vast shed; it's very light, with the sky's expanse visible above.

There's no ceiling, just the sunshine streaming down through the glass roof. Two enormous wooden doors, forming the whole of the far end, open outwards onto a gravelled area towards the sea.

Where she works is almost like working outside as the doors never seem to be closed. They need to be open as the job she does gives off fumes. Her work is interesting. I can walk in and watch. She's always alone; I never see anyone else in this area.

Hanging on the walls around the shed are the different moulds she uses. She doesn't use the big ones of boat hulls; I've never seen them in use. Her moulds are much smaller.

She takes a mould and coats it with a very sticky resin kept in a huge round tin. She carefully places a mat of woven glass strands upon this area and dabs more resin all over; the mat is kept evenly in place this way. Layer by layer, it is built up until it is considered strong.

Released from the mould, it will take the shape of a tea tray; it will be in need of decoration. I'm never there when it is removed from the mould; by the time I reach the shed after school the next day, my mother is onto the next item.

I love the smell of the resin wafting out to greet me when I arrive and the feel of the smooth, woven glass sheets that slide around when I lightly touch the top one on the high pile. A sheet has to be lifted very gently when required, otherwise it could easily fall apart.

The resin's distinctive smell slides up my nostrils in the same way as eucalyptus does when it is put on my pillow by Granny when I have a cold that has blocked my nose. I like smelling both.

This fibreglass is an amazing material; it has so many uses as it's immensely strong when set thickly. I'm told that some car body parts are made of it but it's expensive because the sections are all constructed by hand, exactly the same way as these smaller trays and boxes. The glass sheets have no smell at all; the smell and fumes rise only from the resin pot.

The process is very time-consuming, especially on a large scale, but it has the advantage of taking on any shape required, large or small.

This is better than watching and hearing the poor lobster squeal in his last moments of life when placed in the vat of boiling water.

These fascinating, extraordinary creatures are unloaded from the lobster pots at the jetty and moved straight to the vast tank where they wait to be lifted out to fulfil a customer's order.

E4 Fascinating Artefact

All five of us are invited to play cards tonight.

One of the sisters has her apartment on the ground floor. We play cards on the huge dining table; it has six matching chairs and two carvers, which are each positioned at the long ends of the table.

Going through to the drawing room where the table is, I pass a very special doll's house. It's definitely not homemade; neither does it look played with. It has three storeys with a big staircase; it houses wonderful furniture. The rooms have high ceilings with chandeliers.

I think it is built like a Victorian house for a very large family, with space for servants on the upper floor.

It stands on its own table in the space beneath the wide staircase that goes on up to the other sister's apartment. The steep stairs at the back of the house are those used by us, for visiting the upstairs sister. They aren't visible from in here.

I'd like to have a really close look at the doll's house, but it's in the darkest area of the room and I feel I can only glance in passing; I've not ever been invited to look at it.

Each time I pass, I see something different. I can only imagine the front of the doll's house because if that section exists, it's not on show anywhere.

I'm not sure my two sisters have even noticed the doll's house there. Perhaps they don't find it of any great interest, as I do.

I don't ever draw attention to the fact that I like the house; I first need an indication from the Armstrong sisters that are happy for me to go closer.

I can't say I miss anything back at 6 Ash Close. I've never missed my doll's house, or my favourite books, or even my puppets.

This life in Warsash is different from that life. This is more like being on holiday all the time; we never took such things away on holiday, so it's never felt strange not to have them here.

Granny says, "Out of sight out of mind." I'm pleased to be here and happy that I no longer need the things I used to treasure.

The packs of cards are already on the table, which has a wonderful sheen. I don't expect the sisters would apply polish to their tables; "the fairies" are sent, I suspect.

I'm placed looking across to the space under the stairs; I can see the doll's house, but it's no longer on my mind.

One of the carvers has been brought around from the end to make seven manageable places; we need to reach all the cards that will be set on the table as we play. The object is to get rid of my 13 "demons" which sit in a pile next to me. We race to then shout, "Pounce!"

We call the game Pounce. The sisters call it Racing Demons.

It's a mad rush when we start. We can only see our top demon. The rest are face down.

Quickly we stack our cards in ordered piles spread out on the table. We must be quick if we spot a pile where a demon card can go: someone might get there first!

I'm allowed to stand, otherwise I can't reach the far piles.

I'm quite good at shouting "Pounce" because I'm often faster at getting my cards on the piles than the adults. It's an exciting game and quickly over. Then the shuffling and dealing are done again; I then wait again, poised for the word "Go!"

E5 Life Change

Aunty Jean has returned to Windyridge; it's news to me that this was going to happen.

I'm home from school to find that aunty Jean has gone and now a dog is in the flat. A medium-sized mongrel, dark with a scruffy coat. He's full of life.

My mother once came home with such a dog at 6 Ash Close. He was with us just one day before he was back where he came from, wandering nose to the ground outside, as strays are inclined to do. My father hadn't been happy to see the new arrival.

Any dog that has no collar and is willing to leave the interesting smells of the street to follow my mother home is deemed a stray.

I've come back home from school.

My mouth drops open with shock; then I feel strangely amused. I'm home to find all the living room cushions ripped to pieces. The whole room is white with snowy feathers. Every surface has tiny fluffy down resting upon it.

I can imagine the fun he had, going from one cushion to another. His stay with us will inevitably be a short one; he too will go back where he came from, I guess.

This one has lasted a bit longer; a few weeks longer.

I hear talk that my mother has had "advice". Divorce on grounds of cruelty is not thought to be a good idea, so solicitors tell her. The "respondent", as he is now referred to, could lose his position as senior master at Erith Grammar if she pursues this line of attack in the case process.

If that happened, she would be unlikely to receive any maintenance at all; a different approach is needed, I gather.

The decision has been made: she is to drop her case. By letting time pass, my father will be able to divorce her on grounds of "desertion".

There has to be a three-year period for this to happen; then the "respondent" will be free to file for the divorce, rather than my mother bringing the case to court now.

With no money from my father, there are only my mother's wages on which to live. Three years will be a long time to wait for any awarded maintenance.

My mother is now well behind with the flat's rent at Warsash Court, so we have to move pretty quickly. The Armstrong sisters have done their best, but living rent-free in their flat isn't going to happen, so we will have to leave. My mother, up until now, hasn't been used to finding rent.

Another new life. What now? Where will we go?

Chapter F The Bungalow

F1 Unimagined Gesture

We are on the move today. There's not much to pack.

We walk up the main street towards Locks Heath; we are heading for a side road up on the right with little more to carry than when we arrived at Waterloo Station last summer.

We won't need the tents; they will stay stored in the stables with the piano and the sewing machine. With us, we have the primus, the green enamelled Valor-Perfection stove, the three billy cans for cooking which sit neatly inside one another, and our lilos and sleeping bags.

There won't be furniture or a stove provided, but we will have electricity, a kitchen sink and a bathroom.

The place we are heading for is 1, Osborne Road. It's on an unadopted road off the main street; it sweeps up right around past the church and then out onto the main thoroughfare again but further up towards Locks Heath. It's a very big, looped, gravel road, with individual newly built properties dotted along on the numerous allocated plots. Designed and built by different builders, they all take on variations of form. It's an interesting, quiet road as it doesn't lead onwards anywhere.

Just past a rough site remaining empty on the right, where a home could be built, is our next home. I guess the first patch isn't popular as it's on the corner with the main street.

I can see, as I'm approaching, that the place is low-roofed; a bungalow. There's space in its front area to pull in a car off the gravelled road. Numerous bushes edge the property's boundary, but it has no gates or fences to speak of; it's open right around the bungalow to the rough grass of the ground behind. The back area of the unkempt plot has the addition of two substantial concrete posts erected for the washing line.

It's a new build, standing alone; a bungalow that's never been lived in before.

A young couple who have plans to marry in six months' time own it. Until their wedding day, their new bungalow was to lie empty. We are invited to live here for the six months leading up to their marriage. I fully recognise what a generous gesture this is, handing over their prospective new home to complete strangers. We are to "Christen" it, it would appear.

I blow up my lilo and unroll my sleeping bag, which is somewhat depleted of feathers now. The lilo has sprung leaks over time, but they are quickly patched. By running my hand over the fully blown lilo, I can easily locate the smallest of holes. Wetting my hand first is even better for feeling the escaping air. Each lilo was supplied with a repair kit tied on; they still contain a tiny tube of glue and round patches to match each lilo.

We three girls are to sleep in the large front room. The bushes in the front garden mean we can't be easily seen. There are no curtains, but we are well sheltered from the road. The bushes, already established, were growing here before the gravel road was laid.

The primus stove is set up in the middle of the kitchen, which has its door conveniently opening out near the intended washing line.

Our camping stools have green canvas seats and metal tubular legs, each fixed so the stools can fold up. The two rungs sitting along the ground are bent up to form slight feet. They don't feel secure; they wobble when I lean forward to put down my empty mug on the floor. The stools are to be folded and stacked.

Strong wooden fruit boxes, mainly used for apples and plums, are fetched from the greengrocer. They prove far more stable on the Marley tiles; balancing is no longer required.

We have with us our enamel camping ware; one single plate is sludgy yellow with a green rim. All the rest, the plates and mugs, are white with deep blue rims.

We are camping in the kitchen! I'm happily supping away from my tin mug filled with freshly heated soup; my favourite: Heinz tomato.

Life is good. Very nearby, across the main street, I can take the bus to school. I'm soon to leave Locks Heath Primary to attend Sarisbury Green Secondary

Modern. I shall be able to make my own way on my bicycle.

I won't have this next school to myself, my older sister is already there.

F2 Landscape Creation

With my mind occupied with the thought of exploring, I quickly find a way through the bushes into the vacant plot of land next door. It has far more to offer than our garden, which is little more than rough grass and builders' rubble.

By often walking around the adjoining plot, I find I have beaten a path in the undergrowth. I'm surprised how easily it formed. Nobody from the road can see where I'm heading.

Neither my mother nor my sisters show any desire to join me. I'm happy

for it to be my very own haunt where I can watch out for things and see what plants come up and flower. My trail twists and weaves between the undergrowth; I've created my own world. Being alone and absorbed, I'm very suitably content.

F3 Ambitious Vision

Just across the main road where I catch the bus to school is a small, low building looking much like a very long prefab. It's surrounded by a vast expanse of disused ground with little natural growth. This extends out to the front, providing very suitable parking for large vehicles such as lorries. It serves as a cafe serving snacks of different sorts.

Gravelled areas such as this are prolific around Warsash. The site may have been a levelled-off disused gravel pit.

Emily has recently moved into the cafe. She's my age but attends a different school.

The Anderson family are keen and energetic, with incredible vision.

They've recently arrived from New Zealand; they propose enlarging the cafe and incorporating adequate accommodation for the family. Emily has a younger brother.

A new distinctive sign is up already.

Swinging high, in a strong wooden frame, atop a substantial post, it cannot be missed: Silver Fern Cafe. It depicts just one big fern leaf painted silver on a dark grey background.

The flimsy-looking cafe standing alone doesn't look as if it might offer much in the way of food, but the classy sign indicates otherwise. The scene looks somewhat incongruous, like the railway guard wearing the Coronation crown.

I'm intrigued by the plan and how the work is to progress.

While at the bus stop, I have time to mull over how they intend to achieve their goal. The long, prefab cafe is to stay on the site where the new building is to stand; the cafe must stay open, I hear.

This is not a problem for the Andersons, who are now building the walls of their new building around the old cafe. At the moment, the family are housed in a long caravan parked behind and out of sight.

Stacks of new tiles have arrived. They are unusually green.

When the new roof goes on, the old cafe is still operating but it is incorporated inside the new building!

From the road, you would never guess that the old prefab still exists; that it is still operating inside the new large building. It's an unusual way of doing things; perhaps this is how they would do it in New Zealand if such a problem arose.

When they reach the right moment, the old cafe inside is to be demolished, I hear. In my mind, it will be an enormous task; such an exciting moment though, to bring the old building out in pieces to be taken away.

F4 Uncertain Procedure

Arriving at school today, my class get a big surprise. Our classroom has a scattering of half a dozen or so desks left in it; the rest have been moved to the sides. What's going on?

The 11 Plus!

I won't be included, so I wonder where I will go while the room is in use for the test?

My name is called, so I have to stay in the classroom. Perhaps I can read a book?

No more than a dozen of us take our seats, the rest of my class are younger. It's very interesting because until this moment I didn't have much idea who would be leaving Locks Heath at the end of the summer term; I've not taken notice of the ages of those in my class before.

Most of my class, I now know, are younger and will return here to school. We weren't told when the test was to take place. No practice happened as it did when I was at Wingham School.

Papers are placed before me. Should I tell the teacher that I've already done the 11 Plus?

It will cause a terrible delay to everything. How could it be checked that I had done it already? Who could they ask? I did it miles away in Kent.

I shall do as I'm told. I won't draw attention to it. They can find out later that I've already failed it. If I were to pass this now, I'd be in shock. There's no way I want to go to a grammar school. That would feel like my worst nightmare. I don't think I would ever have time to relax if sent to a grammar school; all heads down, push, push, push. It doesn't feel me; I'm far from being "a swatter". Where is the school? I've no idea!

There are just a few of us here, and I already know only a couple will head to the grammar school, so I don't think I need to worry too much.

With all their heads down, they will be trying to pass. I feel I can relax.

The papers are like the ones I've seen before. Nothing is a surprise.

I go through the tests without a care in the world because I already know what I want. Failure is very much on my mind.

When the results are eventually announced, I will be nervous, even so, because sometimes things are hard to predict.

The thought that I might be asked to take the 11 Plus twice had never crossed my mind. I didn't know it was possible.

F5 Individual Taste

With the upper floor of The Silver Fern in place, complete with a new wide central staircase, I can go upstairs with Emily to visit the vast space they have created.

Up here, rooms are yet to be formed. The large, uninterrupted space echoes as we walk across the bare floorboards. The black roof felt between the rafters is still visible. Dormer windows are up on what might end up as a third floor.

Two large, comfortable armchairs and a large television are the sole items in the space. The television stands alone in prime position.

I'm invited to go over at a particular time after school to watch a programme that Emily loves.

Her younger brother isn't here to watch with us. This programme isn't something I know about, so I'm excited to see it.

We climb the stairs. Emily's mother brings up homemade snacks from the cafe; we eat, curled up in the plush chairs, plates on our knees, patiently waiting for the test card to leave the screen and the programme to begin.

I watch Emily as the programme is due to begin. She is full of anticipation; her eyes light up as soon as the test card goes off the screen. She quickly readjusts her position to feel most comfortable.

Big Ben strikes 6 o'clock. Then a train whistle blows; music slowly builds as a train steams down a track towards us. The driver with his peaked cap is ready to stoke the boiler. Grey smoke billows out around the speeding engine; the whistle blows again. A film of a moving train depicted this way is quite exhilarating. It's an exciting start; I like it.

It reminds me of a poem I learnt in school: "Faster than fairies, faster than witches".

There's an urgency created as in a mystery film at the Odeon; the lion has already roared; the film has begun. Already I'm on the edge of my seat, ready for the unexpected . . . *Murder on the 6.05*, perhaps.

The mood is set, the music fits the speed of the scene superbly, but I still can't guess how the programme will proceed.

I'm here because of Emily; because she was very keen to invite me to join her, for no other reason. When her eyes lit up, I was unexpectedly enveloped by her enthusiasm.

"You must come over and watch, Helen! Please come; it starts at 6 o'clock."

Emily and her family are great, but I'm not so keen on her programme choice.

It started well, but that was just the introduction. I suffered till the end as I didn't want to sound ungrateful after her inviting me.

Rock 'n roll, skiffle boards and loud singing just doesn't appeal to me. It's the other end of the scale from what I'm used to hearing. Quite a contrast to Vaughan Williams with his *Lark Ascending*.

Six-Five Special is a programme I won't be hankering to see again. I've not thought about television for some time now. I can't say I miss such things as *The Brains Trust* and "the cricket", my father's choices.

As with *Six-Five Special*, the best bit of *In Town Tonight* was the very start of the programme; to see the traffic stop on the Hyde Park Corner roundabout!

Jacque Cousteau in his *Silent World* – that would still be my choice, if we had a television now, I think.

F6 Strange Solution

Before we finish school for the summer holidays, a large bucket with a piece of board placed across its top is being carried from class to class. The contents of the bucket are from the waters of the Solent.

Lee-on-Solent is where we go swimming sometimes. Mother insists we swim whatever the weather, even if it's raining. No one else can be seen bobbing up and down on such occasions, only us. It's frequently warmer in than out, which often surprises me. If it's bucketing down with rain, it makes little difference; my mother insists:

"You'll just get a bit wetter than you are, that's all."

The sewage pipe is first viewed and assessed. If it stands too high out of the water, swimming is off the agenda. Rain is fine, but not the pipe showing its broad back with its gurgling contents within.

Down at Windyridge, the farm is not close to the sea like at Lee-on-Solent, so the homes have no such drainage system. Septic tanks and soak-aways are normal in that area, each house having one of its own or perhaps sharing one.

Sometimes the Windyridge soak-away causes a problem. I hear the concern in the adults' voices:

"It's not breaking down. We'll have to throw in a dead chicken."

I know it's not witchcraft I'm listening to. I do wonder what possible good a dead chicken will do when it is thrown into the cesspit. Anyway, why not save the feathers is my question.

"No, it has to be the complete chicken, feathers-n-all."

Now, that really does sound far-fetched!

Ceremoniously, the bucket in school today is being carried around our area of Hampshire to every school. I'm extremely curious. The contents have been recovered from the beach at Lee-on-Solent, rather than from the water.

The man in charge of the bucket is warning us of the dangers we might face if we swim in the seas around the coast at this time.

The description of long stinging tentacles catches my imagination. How many tentacles? How thick? How does the creature know you are near when it is yards away from you in the water? Can it sense your body?

So, they are big but difficult to spot because their large bodies stay mostly below the surface. Like an iceberg, mostly out of view.

This creature is from story books!

"You will be stung badly if the tentacles touch your skin."

I'm so wanting to look in the bucket. Let me see in the bucket! My imagination isn't helping.

Now, at last, it's my turn to look.

It's amazing but evidently dead. He didn't describe the delicate blue colour of its milky glass-like surface. Perfectly shaped like an expensive shade of an oil lamp that defuses the light.

Its big body fills half the bucket; it is without water.

Nobody told us that the creature in the bucket was dead. There are no tentacles that I can see. I'm disappointed by its being stuffed into the bucket in such a way. Perhaps the long tentacles are underneath its translucent body.

Anyway, it's not the man-of-war I was led to expect; it's a very large, but very dead, jellyfish.

"They've come over from Portugal. You must all keep off the beaches."

How amazing; did it swim here? I have no great sense or understanding of anything except the great horror this handler is creating in the classroom.

I'm not scared of it, though. Swimming would be out of the question, but I would dearly like to see a Portuguese man-of-war in the sea, alive.

Home from school, I'm full of excitement.

"Mum, can we go to Lee-on-Solent on Saturday?

F7 Exquisitely Unique

The trail around my plot is in the form of a long snake holding its tail in its mouth; no corners to negotiate but plenty of squiggles this way and that. It takes time to get around as it weaves amongst the bushes.

I'm not far from when the beginning will be in view again. I've reached the section where my trail hugs the taller bushes, skirting the perimeter of the plot along the gravel road.

Glancing ahead where the shade forms, from the top of the bushes down across the path, I see at eye level a white shape on the greenery. It's unusual and puzzling as it's not been there before when I've passed. I know this trail intimately.

Perhaps a small tail feather could be that white, but I can't imagine what bird could lay claim to it; it's too crisp and tiny.

There's no breeze to give the shape motion.

Closer, my eyes and thoughts adjust to its being an insect. I stare with incredulity at the creature that at some time alighted on the deep green laurel leaf, so perfectly positioned for me to study it.

It shows no inclination to move. I'm inches away, with time to study its structure. Few creatures would allow such an intrusion; the grasshopper would spring, the tiny frog leap, the dragonfly dart away.

Would anyone believe me if I was to describe this tiny insect to them? I don't think so. I'm overwhelmed by its delicate, infinitely beautiful structure.

Pure chalk white. A long, thin body as slender as a very small damselfly. A pair of wings, long and outstretched, like the wings on a small plane just landed with perfect precision. Not designed to fold up or lie its wings back. Every part is Omo-bright, not created with camouflage in mind.

It stands out boldly, snow white on the dark green foliage of the laurel, with its thread-fine white legs arranged in a symmetrical pattern.

Its wings are more amazing than anything I have ever seen. When I look closer, they appear to be formed from a few, minute, long feathers.

Stunning, on a bright sunny day, alighting on a conveniently placed landing pad, it was poised, awaiting study by me.

What is this magical creature?

I will keep it in my mind. One day, some day, I must find out.

F8 Unforgivable Outcome

When heading off to Lee-on-Solent for the cinema, we can combine our visit with a swim in the sea.

The weather is immaterial; the state of the tide has to be acceptable, though. Along from the cinema, on the shore side of the street, is the large pipe that runs out into the Solent. It's barely visible at high tide; at low tide, it's another matter. It then looms large like a Loch Ness sea monster slipping out from the sands to find a breakfast snack.

To walk out far across the mud to swim would position swimmers closer to the pipe's large outlet. It's not a nice prospect contemplating what might appear in the water out there! There are numerous pipes of this size along the coast taking people's waste out to sea.

With the area having four tides, due to the Isle of Wight's positioning, I suppose it is considered acceptable practice.

When I'm in the water, I keep my eyes skimming for any undesirables that might be drifting in-shore. It's not unknown.

We shan't be hanging around today; the tide is right, but it's not what one might call "beach weather"; a quick dip before the film and that will be all.

The shore is empty of people, which isn't surprising. We pitch ourselves by our usual breaker, which sometimes acquires a neat slope of pebbles; the slope is never that high, so the thick wooden breaker always affords us some protection from the winds.

While we are busy drying off afterwards, we notice two people wading ashore. None of us were aware that we had company; they must have been swimming further out.

I somehow don't think they noticed the sewer pipe's existence just under the surface. My mother says nothing; it's all a bit late for warning them, I suppose.

Closer, I see it's two chaps, perhaps in their 30s.

They are not yet close enough to greet us. I'm looking, rather rudely, possibly; it's not a sight I've seen here before: two swimmers rising up to come inshore from deserted seas, alone; until then unnoticed.

From the Isle of Wight? Or perhaps France?

Approaching from the shore line both have stopped suddenly. Something appears to have attracted their attention as they are both staring towards the road. I look where they are looking, expecting to see something unusual.

We all look.

Nothing. There's nothing unusual to see.

"All our things are gone, everything!"

They have lost all their clothes, their shoes. I presume their keys and money? The spot where they left them shows no evidence of this meanest of acts. The theft happened before we settled as we saw an empty beach when we got here.

We arrived too late to prevent the deed from happening. What if all our stuff had been stolen?

What a terrible prospect we would have faced. What would we have done?

They walk, barefoot and wet, dressed only in trunks, towards the town centre.

F9 Creating Happiness

Roy and Marjorie Blake live opposite the disused gravel pits on Warsash Common; it's not many minutes on my bicycle from Osborne Road.

Dibles Road is a dead end, so it's a very quiet area; they have a cottage where they live with their three girls, Joyce, Sandra and Ellen. Joyce is a Guider, along with my older sister. It was through my sister that we got to know the family.

The cottage is not far from the end of Dibles Road. I can push my bicycle through the end bollards near their cottage, but no cars can pass through.

They have a large, cultivated back garden with vegetables, flowers and chickens. Nothing appears too precious or regimented, so it's a great garden to explore.

The area of the common over the road is a large expanse with many dips and mounds in the gravel. It's been left to the will of nature for years. The dips retain little water; the gravel drains well. What sustenance there is enables a little vegetation to take hold, mainly a low-flowering ground cover that acts to stabilise the gravel slopes and mounds in the form of a living carpet.

Conditions suit the prolific, hardy sweet pea with its magnificent blooms of magenta, and nasturtiums in deep orange also abound. Blackberries skirt the edges. None of it is contained in any way, so we can freely wander, explore and pick whatever takes our fancy.

The family are all very active around the home, Nothing is over-emphasised as being important or necessary; it's an unseen order that allows life to just flow naturally. It's always a place full of laughter, fun and involvement; I can pop over on my bike, slotting into whatever moment of life has arrived with them. I'm always made very welcome.

Roy lectures at a technical college. Marjorie looks after the daily needs of the family. She's sometimes preserving fruit or making chutney. Sloes are added to gin for Christmas; large demi jars of fermenting wines made from anything that will make wine, from wild fruits to previously brewed tea leaves, line the passage. The feeling is of rural life enjoyed and relished by all. I have plenty of time during the holidays to be there while my mother is at work.

F10 Fulfilled Wish

I arrive to find the wooden chicken houses are the focus of the day. They need to have the floors scraped and the droppings spread around the plants. We younger girls can easily get inside a hen house and so set to work with shovels, trowels and spades.

The chicken coops are on legs with suspended planked floors so the noise of our scraping reverberates around the neighbourhood; it echoes loudly inside the hut, too.

I've borrowed large wellingtons that swamp my feet, so I'm having to shuffle while shovelling the smelly muck. It's not too bad as most of the droppings I come across are dried and crusty.

Where the hens have roosted at night, the muck is thickly piled, yet other areas have very little. I think I could almost have managed without the boots. The more muck in a pile to clear the better. I like it best when I can fill my bucket quickly.

It's now decided that we can have one of the cleaned huts to make into a place for ourselves; a den. The hut chosen is central, amongst the flowers and veg. This one's not surrounded by a chicken-wire fence like the others. We've made our route wind through the Brussels sprouts and lupins, so it is quite well hidden. Our den appears more secret with its path weaving in and out like this.

We are handed lots of things from the house that are past requirements: pots, saucepans and an old flat iron, much rusted but still with a smooth, silky bottom; it keeps the door closed. Wooden fruit boxes are found for us to sit on and a vase for ox-eye daisies, cut from the edge of the pits where they grow profusely.

Marjorie fishes out some material to form curtains for the little window and brings down a rag rug that the family made some years before from lengths of their old cotton frocks. Its multi-coloured material strips are wound around rope and sewn into a coil. It's had some good use; the thick rope is now showing through in places.

The family are all creative. Sandra and Ellen bring knitting and crochet down to the hut; comics and books, too.

Amongst them, I spot some Enid Blyton Magazines, never favoured by my father.

Now I'm smiling; the chicken house is perfect.

F11 Handled Carefully

One of the girls I've been chatting to in my class lives in a caravan. What fun that must be. I've occasionally seen a caravan being pulled along the road when people are off on their holidays; I've never been in one. To actually live in one must be great fun; like being on permanent holiday perhaps? I love that idea.

I've learnt that a girl called Trixie has chickens in her garden and that they run freely during the day-time.

Just like the penned chickens at Windyridge they take themselves into the chicken house at night to roost. She tells me that her family never trained them to do this, they just do it naturally to feel safe at night.

I'm invited to visit Trixie after school to have tea. From her house I can still catch a bus back home.

My visit to Trixie has had to be arranged; it isn't the same as my going to see the Blakes in their home, where I can just turn up when I like and join in with them when they eat. There is never a need for an invitation, arranged in advance.

I don't remember, in my whole life, ever inviting a friend back to where I live, to have tea. This is a new experience, being invited to have tea at a friend's house.

I think it has happened because I'm interested in their chickens. Trixie must have spoken about it to her parents.

Their chickens, I discover, are large with rusty-coloured feathers. To have one of them lifted up into my outstretched arms! What a wonderful suggestion. I've never been offered this anywhere else.

They look so light, dancing about the garden quite fast, squawking to avoid the dog, who is wanting to play.

Placed in my open arms, the chicken's weight is a big surprise. They are not mostly fluffy feathers as I thought; far from it. Before, I only knew of the large bag of feathers that came off just one chicken at Windyridge; how very light it was.

The chicken doesn't struggle. It's as though it is well used to this happening. It appears to trust that I will put it back on the ground when I'm ready.

Being stroked like a cat the chicken is calm and appears to enjoy it.

I eventually bend down to put her back on the ground

It's very quick to leave once its claws touch the hard surface.

I felt the strength of her legs and watched her speed away with apparent relief; adjusting her feathers with a few quick shakes of her body as she went. It appears she hadn't enjoyed her experience in my arms. She's not returning for more and is soon absorbed and is unidentifiable amongst the other look-alikes.

Stroking her cool back feathers at the same time as feeling the warmth of her belly through my clothes like a hot water bottle was an amazing surprise. Warmth from her could be felt immediately, as soon as the chicken's chest was pressed up close to mine.

The way they prance daintily about on their thin yellow legs is very deceptive. Those legs are extremely strong; made to support a deceptively hefty body. Our eyes see, but what we think is not always the truth.

It comes as a shock, sometimes, when things we think we know don't match up with reality; yet the surprise can have a strange delight to it, knowing that it has been kept a perfect secret from you, until the moment when you discover the truth.

F12 Mystery Guest?

On arriving home from school, I find a car pulled off the road in front of number 1. It's large, partly timbered like the Morris Traveller, but quite a bit bigger. It's not a vehicle I recognize, so I can't guess who the visitor might be.

My mother arranged delivery of this car, it would seem. It's a Morris Oxford. She approached Mercantile Credit, who had "put up" the money. This is how she explains its being here.

We are soon all aboard to be driven out and about.

Great day trips abound, locally: Lee-on-Solent, Hill Head, Droxford, Hedge End, Nunney. It's an old car, but it gets us to where we choose to go, and back. There are trips to Fareham for films at the Odeon and Hill Head for the beach.

Having a motor car has certainly expanded our perimeters; we've been further down local lanes than we ever have by walking or cycling. I love the Floating Bridge in Woolston; we've done that trip several times.

Waiting our turn, I watch the two bridges float past each other in the middle of the river. Each of the ferries can take perhaps a dozen cars, but it's never that busy when we go to cross.

Once on board, I get out of the car and stand by the ferry's side rails where I hear the bell ring to announce our departure; I watch the drawbridge being raised slightly and listen to the strong, heavy chains as they move us out into the deeper water. I love this type of crossing more than any other. It might not look as though we can reach the other shore as we float skew-whiff in the river, but the chains keep us on track and stop us drifting. We are pulled or pushed by the tide but always come right in the end; the massive chains are working out of sight.

Gosport Floating Bridge is worked in a similar way and is another exciting trip across a river by car or on foot. It's always busy with people, cars, motorbikes and sometimes sidecars. Gulls dive and squawk overhead, hoping for fish to surface in the squall of water.

I like visiting Hamble, but it's better to get there by small boat as it takes no time at all. There's a place on the Warsash side of the Hamble River where you can stand and be seen waving. It's just along the road from where we got the clay for baking our pots in the kiln when camping.

Someone might spot our arms flapping from this unlikely, isolated spot, and if we're lucky, the rowing boat will leave the far bank. It takes time to reach us as it never travels in a straight line. The skipper rows up the river as he's coming across so that the river's flow doesn't take him out to sea. The boatman knows the strength of the tide, however high or low it is, and takes his boat up higher or lower accordingly.

While standing on the little jetty, we have a view up the river of a large vessel painted black and white. It's out in the water permanently moored. From where we are, it seems to be just the hull of a ship with gun portals in its lower flanks. It's reminiscent of *HMS Victory*'s hull in Portsmouth. I gather from local people that it's a training ship called the *Mercury*.

Further downriver past Warsash Court is the Naval College, so I expect it is connected to that. Occasionally I've seen small boats pull alongside the hull, dwarfed by its size, and tiny people climb from the boat and disappear in through the side of the hull.

If we are patient, the rowing boat will come once we are spotted. I think it must take time for the boatman to be fetched from his work by whoever sees us all waving. It's best not to give up too early. He will come if he is in the area.

Five in the boat is enough.

We've never met any other passengers either going or coming back; it's like our very own private service hailed whenever we need it. We are rarely disappointed, normally making it across as planned.

The return crossing is never a consideration. It's a foregone conclusion that somehow we will be returned to our riverbank later.

F13 Loading Exercise

Arriving home from school today, I'm just in time to see the Morris Oxford going slowly up the ramp of a low-loader from its usual position near our front door. It's rather amusing to see it creeping up the slope with nobody in it, not even a driver.

I look on, feeling surprised and puzzled as there had been no mention of this going to happen. The men do not acknowledge me, nor do I speak to them. The three talk amongst themselves until the car reaches the level platform of the lorry. Then, with the tailgate lifted, they are quickly away.

Ten minutes later and I would have missed seeing this event taking place. I wonder why they didn't drive it away? Coming with a large vehicle to move a car that works makes little sense that I can see.

Its stay with us was short and sweet, but it was good while it lasted.

My mother shows no surprise to find the empty space. Not thieves then; she knew this was to happen? It went, she says, because the "agreement was not kept".

My mother broke her promise to pay the instalments to the credit company, I gather.

We will soon near the end of our six-month stay here at 1 Osborne Road. I'm feeling anxious about my mother's promise to the couple. What if she plans not to move us out when the time arrives?

My biggest fear is that she will not stick to her agreement with the couple; that she will let them down on their wedding day.

I'll try to put it out of my mind as there's nothing I can do about what my mother does or does not do.

F14 Interpreted Situation

I'm in the bungalow alone, busy looking through my *Observer Book of Trees*. Through the window of the front room, I see a man approaching the front door from the gravel road.

Part of his attire I can see clearly: a white dog collar; it's the vicar. I open the front door to him, still holding my book; I'm wondering what his visit can be about. Nobody has ever come knocking here before, not even the postman.

The vicar carries something in his hand.

"We would like your family to have this, a gift from our Harvest Festival."

I thank him and watch him turn and go. I look down at the packet he handed me; I'm a little puzzled. It's a 2lb bag of Tate and Lyle sugar. How kind that he should be thinking of us when so many people live in Warsash.

I'm thinking: we must be considered poor.

This is the first time I've given any thought to the idea that we are poor. What is it to be: "in poverty"? Why haven't I felt it? How can I be poor if I'm very happy? I want him to come back so that I can tell him that I am happy being "poor".

My thoughts have turned to pancakes with squeezed lemon and sugar . . . not just one!

F15 Dogid Determination

I was enrolled as a Brownie while I was at Ash Close before I joined the Warsash Brownies. My mother and her three siblings had all been ardent Girl Guides till they became too old and had to leave.

Their reminiscing about the flag being raised up a pole at guide camp and the Queen's Guide award attained by my Aunty Jean fired my imagination.

At Windyridge there are marvellous pictures of the sisters together with Pixie, my mother's best school friend, outside their big round tent at Guide camp: calf-length skirts, white lanyards and dark-brimmed hats.

I couldn't wait to be old enough to be a Guide myself; it all looked and felt so exciting.

I was an equally ardent Brownie once I joined, doing all the activities required to get the embroidered badges to sew on the sleeve of my short cotton Brownie tunic.

I proudly ironed my lovely yellow tie and folded it in a very special way before tying it round my neck. If ever the need arose, I knew how to unfold it and make a sling for a broken arm; I already had my badge for first aid sewn on my sleeve.

Each badge had an embroidered symbol, things like a saucepan for cooking or a cup and saucer for being able to make and serve tea.

My sights were always on reaching the Guides and Guide camp.

Brownies had to come first, though, with Brown Owl and Tawny Owl leading our pack. I was a member of the Robins team. I would never miss it if I could help it. Getting enrolled, learning the Brownie Promise to honour and obey and learning the correct way to salute would be my passport into the Guides one day, I hoped.

Now a guide, in the same arrangement of uniform as my older sister, I feel much like a clone. It's the black hair and the fact that she's short too, that does it.

Parade Day is always one for marching, Brownies and Guides all together. The huge unfurled flag, scrumptiously embroidered, is propped steadily in a lucky Guide's holstered belt as she leads the way up the aisle of the church.

The Brownies don't have pride of place at the front of the procession; that is left for the Guides.

The church, where the parade is held, is towards Sarisbury Green. This will be my first parade as a Guide. I'm in my new blue uniform, red tie and white lanyard with a sparkling whistle on the end. I've no badges on my arm yet, except for the one that states my division.

The church is near my school in Sarisbury so I can now cycle there for Parade Day, as a Girl Guide.

I'm all prepared to leave, but I'm being delayed. If I can't go soon, I will be late.

At last, I'm able to set off.

I pedal as fast as I can; I'm determined I will get there, even if it means missing some of the parade, which starts in the road where everyone congregates; then the parade moves through the church gates and up the path into the church.

Just around this next bend, I will see the church come into view at last. I see no one around; everywhere is quiet. I know this is the right day, so I keep pedalling.

Through the lychgate, I throw my bike down on the grass and burst into the church; they are all calmly seating themselves. At least I've arrived before the service starts.

Out of breath, I squeeze past people to reach a seat at the back, relieved that my efforts have not been in vain. I had to pedal really hard, but I made it; I'm here.

Very soon, I have my head pushed down between my knees by a pair of strong arms. I won't see much of the service this way, but I think I've been saved from "passing out".

I hear muffled whispers around me:

"She came up from Warsash on her bicycle. She rode too hard."

F16 Green Environment

I don't know what to expect when I turn up at my new school today – Sarisbury Green Secondary Modern.

The distance from Osborne Road is under two miles, so it was easy enough to cycle here. I wheel my bike up into the bike shed; I find it's completely open except for the long, solid back wall and the roof. It's designed to keep the bikes dry yet make them easy to take out. It's not what one would think of as a "shed".

Some twenty bikes are already parked up neatly in a row.

As I approach, I see that older children are chatting together behind it, mostly out of sight until I get closer. They are catching up or else, I guess, they are smoking. I tried it once with some boys at junior school; after much coughing and spluttering, I decided it wasn't for me. The boys said it takes time to get the hang of it.

My mother has the hang of it, but she's a "social smoker" she tells me. I only ever used to see her smoke when she was in the front room at Ash Close entertaining friends, with my father also present, but he didn't smoke.

My mother has not smoked since, not even socially when we had tea with the Armstrongs.

The rough path around to the back of the long shed is well-trodden; it looks as though it gets plenty of use for purposes other than school.

There seems to be no uniform. I don't know whether there is one. If there is, I don't see anyone wearing it.

There are a great many boys and girls to get sorted into their correct forms and dispatched to their rooms; there's a certain buzz of excitement in their voices, which reminds me of the children outside the cinema in Petts Wood. I never did get to join them on Saturday mornings.

There's a lot going on. I'll follow the smaller pupils to see where they go. They are heading for the canteen. All the first-year intake are to collect in this large space; the rest of the school already know their classroom position. We will all get allocated a form room and teacher eventually, I gather.

Classrooms are clustered around the open square area that they call the quadrangle. The classroom doors open onto a covered walkway running all the way around the quadrangle, so if it rains, we walk around keeping our books dry. There are pillars to support the canopy, rather than walls, and we are free to cross the open paved space. It reminds me of cloisters in an abbey but without the reverential atmosphere and echoing chanting.

Some rooms have a particular purpose; the art room is opposite my form room across the "quad". There are other single-storey classrooms built outside this main block — Science, Woodwork and Domestic Science rooms that all double up as form rooms for registration.

F17 Puzzle Complete

One of the joys, I discover, will be learning Technical Drawing. We will learn how to precisely represent objects using a sharp pencil and ruler; the paper placed on an angled worktop in front of us. I love the idea of the exactness of the work; it's just up my street and the setup of the room is so "grown-up".

We are to use special small metal rulers in technical drawing so that the sharp point of the pencil tucks tightly into its edge. A metal pencil sharpener each is essential, but there is a robust sharpener clamped to the teacher's desk if you forget to bring your own. This large one has a box to catch the shavings: it has a glass window so that anyone can see if it needs emptying.

I'm hoping Technical Drawing will lead to the chance to do Woodwork in yet another room I've discovered exists.

I soon learn that there are lunchtime clubs. I will attend an art club as soon as I can, and a chess club, too.

In Needlework, we are each to make similar embroidered aprons for our Domestic Science classes which start next term. They are to be in blue, red or green gingham-check with cross-stitch patterning along the seams; I will love doing that.

Field Studies sound very interesting. I wonder what that means. The days will be packed; I can see that.

Each lesson grips me; they are all so different. Chemistry, Biology, Drama, Geography and History. Many more, too. French will start next term, along with Domestic Science, where I will wear the apron I am carefully making in Needlework.

I could never have dreamt of a school like this. It's a perfect place. I'm in my element here.

This could be an opportunity to find out what insect it was that landed in my plot next door. I seek out a teacher; I hope they might know. He tells me straight away:

"That would have been a Plume Moth."

Wonderful! Such an apt name for the exotic feathered insect I saw; the teacher didn't even have to look it up. I'm so impressed.

I'm going to love this place, I can tell. I feel very lucky to be here.

F18 Requested Opinion

Our outing to Fareham this time is not to go to the cinema; we are going to the Courts. We all have to attend.

This won't be the divorce as that won't happen for another two years. This is to do with "custody": who will "get it". I can't say I know what it all means, because I don't.

The Court is held in the sort of building that might be a Town Hall: towering and impressive.

We three children are shown where to sit in a high-ceilinged corridor with coloured floor tiles. There are low windows all along the outside wall. The long green leather seating with padded back and wooden arms reminds me of the ladies' waiting room at the railway station. The exposed wood is more elaborate, but basically it is the same long seat, sturdy and serviceable, made for a public building.

We sit and wait. Time passes; it looks as though we weren't needed after all.

Then I'm shown on my own to a room like an office with a substantial dark wooden desk. I stand; the man seated, facing me directly behind the desk, says:

"Which parent do you want to live with?"

I'm taken aback at being asked such a direct question. Would my answer make any difference, I wonder?

Should I understand from such a question that both my parents want me to live with them? I know my mother doesn't want me to live with my father, but I have no idea whether my father wants me to live with him.

I have no idea what my father is thinking or what he wants.

However, when my mother went into Maidstone Asylum, he sent me to live at Bickley.

He kept my older sister at home, so I guess he would like to have her live with him. She had also passed part one of her 11 Plus, whereas I must have disappointed him with my result.

My younger sister is pernickety with what she will eat, so would he want that bother? She's dead skinny and doesn't like many foods; she is happy to live on salad cream sandwiches. Yuk!

Has she been asked this question too? I guess we all have. It may mean we get split up, I suppose.

I'm enjoying my new school immensely, and also the Guides, so if I can keep both of these, I'll be happy.

I have no need to hesitate; I know my answer:

"My mother."

And so it is. We are all heading back to Osborne Road on the bus.

My mother has made plans to leave Osborne Road; it's a great relief to know she is keeping her promise to find somewhere else to go when our six months in the bungalow are over.

F19 Farewell Warsash

To learn we are not staying in this area is a bitter blow.

It's not that I've made really firm friends with anyone, I haven't. One friend at Locks Heath was Trixie, but she's now at a secondary school towards Fareham. I visited her home occasionally when we were in the same class.

With all the activities during lunch times, I've not had the time to find a particular friend at this school, so friends are not what I will miss.

I will find Guides again, I don't doubt, but I'm having to say goodbye to my wonderful school. It does not feel good at all. My place of inspiration has lasted just one term.